KNOWING THE LIVING

GOD

PAUL DAVID WASHER

KNOWING THE LIVING **GOD**

Published by:

HeartCry Missionary Society
PO Box 3506
Radford, VA 24143

www.heartcrymissionary.com

Printed in the United States of America 2019
Third Edition

Unless otherwise noted, all Scripture quotations taken from the
New American Standard Bible®
Copyright 1960, 1962, 1963, 1968, 1971, 1972, 1973, 1975, 1977, 1995
by the Lockman Foundation. Used by permission.

Edited by Forrest Hite, Meghan Nash, and Elzeline Hite
Layout and design by Jon Green, Matthew Robinson, Forrest Hite, and Michael Reece

KNOWING THE LIVING GOD

Table of Contents

KNOWING THE LIVING GOD

Introduction

METHOD OF STUDY

The great goal of this study is for the student to have an encounter with God through His Word. Founded upon the conviction that the Scriptures are the inspired and infallible Word of God, this study has been designed in such a way that it is literally impossible for the student to advance without an open Bible before him or her. The goal is to help the reader to obey the exhortation of the Apostle Paul in II Timothy 2:15:

> *"Be diligent to present yourself approved to God as a workman who does not need to be ashamed, accurately handling the word of truth."*

Each chapter deals specifically with an aspect of the nature and work of God. The student will complete each chapter by answering the questions and following the instructions according to the Scriptures given. The student is encouraged to meditate upon each text and write his or her thoughts. The benefit gained from this study will depend directly upon the level of the student's investment. If the student answers the questions thoughtlessly, merely copying the text without seeking to discern its meaning, this book will be of very little help.

Knowing the Living God is primarily a biblical study and does not contain much in the way of colorful illustrations, quaint stories, or even theological commentaries. It was the desire of the author to provide a work that simply points the way to the Scriptures and allows the Word of God to speak for itself.

This workbook may be used by an individual, small group, or Sunday school class. It is highly recommended that the student complete each chapter on his or her own before meeting for discussion and questions with the group or discipleship leader.

EXHORTATION TO THE STUDENT

The student is encouraged to study biblical doctrine and discover its exalted place in the Christian life. The true Christian cannot bear or even survive a divorce between the emotions and the intellect or between devotion to God and the doctrine of God. According to the Scriptures, neither our emotions nor our experiences provide an adequate foundation for the Christian life. Only the truths of Scripture, understood with the mind and communicated through doctrine, can provide that sure foundation upon which we should establish our beliefs and our behavior and determine the validity of our emotions and experiences. The mind is not the enemy of the heart, and doctrine is not an obstacle to devotion. The two are indispensable and should be inseparable. The Scriptures command us to love the Lord our God with all our heart, with all our soul, and with all our mind (Matthew 22:37) and to worship God in both spirit and in truth (John 4:24).

The study of doctrine is both an intellectual and devotional discipline. It is a passionate search for God that should always lead the student to greater personal transformation, obedience, and heartfelt worship. Therefore, the student should be on guard against the great error of seeking only impersonal knowledge instead of the person of God. Neither mindless devotion nor mere intellectual pursuits are profitable, for in either case, God is lost.

THE NEW AMERICAN STANDARD BIBLE

The New American Standard Bible is required to complete this study. This version of Scripture was chosen for the following reasons: (1) the unwavering conviction of its translators that the Bible is the infallible Word of God; and (2) its faithfulness to the original languages.

A WORD FROM THE AUTHOR

How can any man or angel write an adequate book on the subject of God Himself? It would be an easier task to count every star in the heavens! With this in mind, I acknowledge that whatever is found to be holy, good, or helpful in these pages is the result of the grace of God alone. Knowing something of the weightiness of the subject matter, I have written this workbook with fear and trembling, considering the words penned in James 3:1:

> "Not many of you should become teachers, my brothers, for you know
> that we who teach will be judged with greater strictness."

I would like to thank my wife Charo, who is growing to be "strong in the Lord," and my four children, who are able to pull me away from my work with a glance. I would also like to thank HeartCry staff member Forrest Hite for his diligent and meticulous editing of the several different manuscripts that he has received. His contributions to the arrangement and overall readability of this work are as significant as they are appreciated. My thanks also are extended to the entire staff at HeartCry, who have been a great encouragement throughout the process of this book's publication, and to Pastor Charles Leiter of Kirksville, Missouri, whose insights were invaluable.

A WORD FROM THE EDITOR

Knowing the Living God is derived from Paul Washer's previously published work, *The One True God*; it has been massively expanded, revised, and modified. Due to the close relationship between the two books, those who have studied *The One True God* will likely recognize some of the material in this workbook. Portions of it are relatively untouched (*e.g.* Chapters 10-14, 48), while some of it is brand new (*e.g.* Chapters 1-2, 4, 42-47), but most of it falls between these extremes. It is my belief that *Knowing the Living God* will prove beneficial to all, regardless of familiarity with *The One True God*.

RECOMMENDED RESOURCES FOR FURTHER STUDIES

The Attributes of God by A.W. Pink
The Knowledge of the Holy by A.W. Tozer
Knowing God by J.I. Packer
The Existence and Attributes of God by Stephen Charnock
Theology Explained and Defended by Timothy Dwight
Behold Your God: Rethinking God Biblically [workbook and DVD series] by John Snyder
The Holiness of God [workbook and DVD series] by R.C. Sproul
The Attributes of God [teaching series] by R.C. Sproul
The Doctrine of God by John Frame (for advanced students)

ADDITIONAL NOTE

You may have noticed that this book is being sold at a strange price. Here's why: one dollar ($) from every copy sold will go directly to fund mission work through HeartCry Missionary Society (heartcrymissionary.com). The rest of the sale price is just enough to cover the cost of printing, publication, and distribution. The author is not profiting from the sale of this book, nor has he profited from the sale of any other book. Over the years, we have utilized and explored many avenues in order to publish these workbooks. Ultimately, we have reached the conclusion that doing so in-house at a low cost, even with slightly lower quality, is the most effective way of getting these useful tools into the hands of as many people across the globe as possible. We hope and pray that the Lord continues to use these books to point His people to His Word unto the edification of His Church.

Optional Study Schedule

Week One: The Knowledge of God and the Doctrine of the Trinity
Day 1:   Chapter 1
Day 2:   Chapter 2, Section 1
Day 3:   Chapter 2, Section 2
Day 4:   Chapter 3
Day 5:   Chapter 4

Week Two: The Nature of God
Day 1:   Chapter 5
Day 2:   Chapter 6, Sections 1-2
Day 3:   Chapter 6, Section 3
Day 4:   Chapter 7, Main Points 1-5
Day 5:   Chapter 7, Main Points 6-10

Week Three: The Excellencies of God, Part 1
Day 1:   Chapter 8
         Chapter 9, Section 1
Day 2:   Chapter 9, Section 2
Day 3:   Chapter 10, Main Points 1-3
Day 4:   Chapter 10, Main Point 4
         Chapter 11
Day 5:   Chapter 12

Week Four: The Excellencies of God, Part 2
Day 1:   Chapter 13, Main Points 1-3
Day 2:   Chapter 13, Main Points 4-6
Day 3:   Chapter 14
Day 4:   Chapter 15, Main Points 1-5
Day 5:   Chapter 15, Main Points 6-8

Week Five: The Holiness and Righteousness of God
Day 1:   Chapter 16, Section 1
         Chapter 16, Section 2, Main Points 1-3
Day 2:   Chapter 16, Section 2, Main Point 4
         Chapter 17, Section 1
         Chapter 17, Section 2, Subsection 1
Day 3:   Chapter 17, Section 2, Subsections 2-3
Day 4:   Chapter 18
Day 5:   Chapter 19

Week Six: The One True God
Day 1:   Chapter 20, Main Points 1-3
Day 2:   Chapter 20, Main Points 4-6
Day 3:   Chapter 21
Day 4:   Chapter 22, Sections 1-2
Day 5:   Chapter 22, Sections 3-4

Week Seven: The Faithfulness of God

Week Eight: The Love of God

Week Nine: God the Creator

Week Ten: God the Sovereign

Week Eleven: God the Lawgiver and Judge

Week Twelve: God the Savior, Part 1

Week Thirteen: God the Savior, Part 2

KNOWING THE LIVING GOD

Chapter 1: The Knowledge of God

THE GREATEST OF ALL KNOWLEDGE

Where should a believer begin his or her study of Christianity? The answer is simple, though not always obvious to all: Christianity is first and foremost about the person and work of God. Therefore, we should begin our study with Him!

1. According to Jeremiah 9:23-24, what is the most important and most essential knowledge that a person can possess? Explain your answer.

_____

_____

_____

_____

_____

_____

NOTES: The attributes of God refer to His fundamental, permanent, and unchanging characteristics—who He really is. It should be obvious that knowledge of God is the most important knowledge that we can possess. As Christians, we should devote our lives to knowing God and making Him known.

2. The knowledge of God begins with His attributes, but does not stop there. It also includes the knowledge of His will. What does Ephesians 5:17 admonish us with regard to this truth?

   a. *So then do not be F_____, but U_____ what the*

   W_____ of the Lord is.

   NOTES: The will of God refers to His purposes, plans, and desires. We are called to seek God's will and live according to it. In the Scriptures, the word "fool" is a moral term. It does not refer to a person who is unintelligent, but to someone who does not recognize the importance of knowing God and living according to His will.

3. According to the words of Jesus in John 17:3, what is eternal life? What is the one great purpose of the believer's new relationship with God?

_____

_____

_____

_____

_____

_____

NOTES: Eternal life does not just refer to a quantity of life (*i.e.* life without end), but to a quality of life: the great purpose of life is to **know God** in an intimate relationship.

BENEFITS OF KNOWING GOD

The benefits of knowing God are so vast that they cannot be considered in detail in this work. However, we will mention a few of the most basic ones that are directly stated in the Scriptures. In the following are found four great benefits that are derived from a biblical knowledge of God.

1. UNDERSTANDING

   a. *What does Proverbs 9:10 teach us about the knowledge of God?*

   (1) The fear of the LORD is the beginning of W_____, and the knowledge

   of the Holy One is U_____.

   NOTES: A correct view of God is necessary in order to have a correct view of everything else. Only in the light of a true knowledge of God can we have a true understanding of reality; especially regarding who we are, our need, and the purpose of our existence.

2. TRUST OR FAITH

   a. *What does Psalm 9:10 say about those who know God?*

   (1) Those who know Your N_____ will put their T_____ in You, for You, O LORD, have not forsaken those who seek You.

NOTES: In the Scriptures, the **name** of God is a reference to God Himself. The more we know about Him (His perfect character and unlimited power), the more we will be able to believe Him and trust Him with every aspect of our lives.

3. SPIRITUAL STRENGTH

   a. *What does Daniel 11:32 teach us about those who know God?*

   (1) The people who know their God will display S_____ and take

   A_____.

   NOTES: To live the Christian life takes a strength that is beyond our own. The more we know about God, the stronger we will be spiritually, and the more willing and able we will be to actively live for Him regardless of the obstacles. The Bible says that in a time of great trial, David "was greatly distressed," but he "strengthened himself in the LORD his God" (I Samuel 30:6).

4. PERSEVERANCE

   a. *In II Timothy 1:12, what declaration does the Apostle Paul make?*

   (1) For this reason I also suffer these things, but I am not ashamed; for I K_____

   whom I have believed and I am C_____ that He is able to guard

   what I have entrusted to Him until that day.

   NOTES: The Apostle Paul wrote this right before he was to die as a martyr for Christ under the corrupt rule of the Roman Empire. He remained faithful to Christ and did not deny the faith. He stood bold, unashamed, and confident because he **knew** the character and power of the One in whom he had come to believe!

DANGERS OF NOT KNOWING GOD

Like the benefits of knowing God, the devastating consequences of not knowing Him are also so vast that they cannot all be considered in detail in this work. However, we will mention six of the most basic, each of which is directly stated in the Scriptures.

1. REMAKING GOD IN OUR OWN IMAGE

   a. *According to Psalm 50:21, what mistake did the Israelites make in their view of God?*

(1) These things you have done and I kept silence; you T_____ that I was

just L_____ you; I will R_____ you and state the case in order

before your eyes.

NOTES: In the absence of a true knowledge of God, man will form his own opinions and remake God in his own image. It will always result in a deformed and degraded view of God. It will always result in God's judgment!

2. FALSE WORSHIP

a. *In John 4:22, what did Jesus tell the Samaritan woman at Jacob's well regarding herself, her people, and their religion?*

(1) You W_____ what you do not K_____.

NOTES: Idolatry occurs whenever we worship anything or anyone other than the living God. In the absence of the true knowledge of God, even those who identify themselves with Christianity are subject to this error. They make a false god in their own mind, and then they worship the god they have made!

3. UNBELIEF OR LACK OF TRUST

a. *In Romans 10:14, what are the implications of the Apostle Paul's questions with regard to knowing God?*

(1) How then will they call on Him in whom they have not believed? How will they

B_____ in Him whom they have not H_____? And

how will they hear without a preacher?

NOTES: Although this text applies directly to the preaching of the gospel, it has a wider application with regard to the knowledge of God—how can one believe in the God who he do not know? This applies not only to the sinner's faith leading to salvation, but also to the believer's faith or trust in God that is necessary to live the Christian life. As we have already learned from Psalm 9:10, only those who know God's name will put their trust in Him.

4. AN INDIFFERENT OR APATHETIC VIEW OF SIN – In I Corinthians 15:34, the Apostle Paul rebuked the church in Corinth because some professing believers among them had no real knowledge of God. This ignorance of God resulted in two dangerous and shameful consequences.

a. *They were not S_____-M_____ as they should have been.* The command, "Become sober-minded," can also be translated, "Sober up" (NET) or "Wake up from your drunken stupor" (ESV). Because they did not know God, they were living like sleeping or drunken men with regard to the dangers of sin and the importance of living according to God's will.

b. *They were S_____.* This comes from the Greek word **hamartánō**, which means, "to miss the mark." Because they missed the mark regarding the nature of God (He is righteous), they also missed the mark regarding how they should live before Him (righteously).

5. LAWLESSNESS – The word "lawlessness" refers to the state of living apart from the law or will of God. It is living as though God had no law or had never given His law to men. It is one of the most grievous consequences of an ignorance of God.

   a. *What insight does Proverbs 29:18 provide with regard to the consequences of a lack of knowledge of God?*

      (1) Where there is no V_____, the people are unrestrained, but

         H_____ is he who keeps the law.

         NOTES: In this context, the word "vision" does not refer to a supernatural dream or vision but to the revelation of God's person and will through the Scriptures. Where there is an ignorance of God's nature and law, the people are unrestrained. The word "unrestrained" comes from a Hebrew word **para**, which means, "to let loose from restraint" or "to act as leader." Those who have no knowledge of God or His will run unrestrained in sin and act as self-appointed leaders apart from God. We find an example of this in the book of Judges: "In those days there was no king in Israel; every man did what was right in his own eyes" (17:6; 21:25).

   b. *In Hosea 4:1-2, the Lord rebukes the nation of Israel for its ignorance of God and describes the kind of lawlessness that always accompanies or is the result of such ignorance. List the specific sins.*

      (1) No F_____ (v.1).

      (2) No K_____ (v.1).

      (3) S_____ (v.2).

      (4) D_____ (v.2).

      (5) M_____ (v.2).

      (6) S_____ (v.2).

      (7) A_____ (v.2).

      (8) V_____ (v.2).

NOTES: Do you see any parallels between the sins that were found in Israel because of their ignorance of God and the behavior of our own society? God's law does not change, and man's sinfulness does not fade. The more we reject the knowledge of God, the more unrestrained and immoral we become!

6. DIVINE JUDGMENT AND DESTRUCTION – This is the most frightening consequence of an ignorance of God. What do the following texts teach us about this truth?

a. *Hosea 4:6*

_____

_____

_____

_____

_____

NOTES: The lack of the knowledge of God is devastating. It leads to being rejected as an instrument of God and to the eventual destruction of individuals and societies. Our ignorance of God will even have a devastating effect upon the generations that follow us.

b. *Romans 1:18*

_____

_____

_____

_____

_____

NOTES: The wrath of God refers to His righteous anger or indignation against sinful men. It is important to note that man is not a victim. The Bible teaches that fallen man is a hater of God (Romans 1:30) and hostile to His law (Romans 8:7). It is because of man's ungodliness and unrighteousness that he rejects, ignores, and even suppresses the truth about God's nature and will.

Chapter 2: Growing in the Knowledge of God

HOW THEN SHALL WE LIVE?

Having witnessed the great importance that the Scriptures give to knowing God, we must ask ourselves: "How then shall we live?" or "What should be our proper response?" We must always remember that in the Christian life we are concerned not only about what we know, but also about how we live in light of what we know!

1. Psalm 105:4-5 contains a powerful and beautiful admonition to seek the Lord. Carefully consider the text; then write your thoughts. How can we apply this admonition to our lives?

_____

_____

_____

_____

_____

2. It is not enough to **begin** seeking the Lord; it must become the life-long practice of our lives. What does Hosea 6:3 admonish us regarding this truth, and what does it promise to all who persevere to know the Lord?

_____

_____

_____

_____

_____

NOTES: The phrase "press on" comes from the Hebrew word **radaf**, which means, "to follow after, run after, pursue, or chase." We are not to be casual or apathetic in our pursuit of the person and will of God, but determined and active—even ambitious.

3. God not only commands us to seek Him, but He has also given us many great and precious promises to encourage us. In Proverbs 2:2-5 is found one of the most powerful promises in the Scriptures regarding the knowledge of God. Consider the text, and write your thoughts.

_____

_____

_____

_____

_____

NOTES: There is an inseparable relationship between the Scriptures and prayer. We are to lift our voice to God in prayer that He might grant us knowledge of Himself and understanding of His will. We are also to seek this knowledge as we would seek silver and hidden treasure in a deep cavern or mine. Notice also that there is a direct relationship between the knowledge of God and our reverence or fear of God. The more we know Him, the more we will respect and honor Him with our lives.

4. According to the following texts from the Scriptures, what is one of the most obvious characteristics of the righteous (those who live in a right relationship with God)?

   a. *Psalm 27:8*

   _____

   _____

   _____

   _____

   b. *Philippians 3:7-8*

   _____

   _____

_____

_____

_____

NOTES: One of the most obvious characteristics of the righteous is that they seek to know God and His will. Although even the most mature and zealous believers will struggle with sin and apathy, we must all press on to know God. To know Him and please Him should be our magnificent obsession and the controlling truth of our lives.

5. According to the following texts from Scriptures, what is one of the most obvious characteristics of the wicked?

   a. *Job 21:14-15*

   _____

   _____

   _____

   _____

   _____

   b. *Psalm 14:1-3*

   _____

   _____

   _____

   _____

   _____

NOTES: We must always remember that we once *were* the persons described in Job 21:14-15 and Psalm 14:1-3, and we would have continued to be so, except for the grace of God. We now love Him because He loved us first (I John 4:19); we did not seek Him, but He sought us (Romans 3:11; Luke 15:1-10); we did not choose Him, but

He chose us (John 15:16)! Whatever good we might do and whatever desire we have for God, it is the result of God's work in us (Ephesians 2:10)! Therefore, "Let him who boasts, boast in the Lord" (I Corinthians 1:31).

THE GREAT SOURCE OF KNOWLEDGE

We have now learned three important truths: God admonishes us to seek Him, He has promised to reveal Himself to those who do seek Him, and the righteous will seek Him. These are great truths; however, one more question remains: "How are we to seek the knowledge of God?" The answer is foundational to the Christian life: we seek the knowledge of God through prayerful study of the Word of God—the Scriptures. We will study this truth in greater depth in later chapters; however, at this point, the most important truth to be gleaned is that the Scriptures are the believer's **one great source** of the knowledge of God.

1. According to the following texts, why are the Scriptures the only truly trustworthy source of the knowledge of God?

   a. *What does II Timothy 3:16 declare about the Scriptures?*

      (1) A_____ Scripture is I_____ by God and profitable for teaching, for reproof, for correction, for training in righteousness.

      NOTES: The word "inspired" literally means, "God-breathed." It is translated from the Greek word **theópneustos** [**theós** = God + **pnéō** = to breathe]. The adjective "all" is also very important. The totality of the Scriptures is from the mouth of God and is therefore without error and entirely trustworthy.

   b. *What does Psalm 12:6 declare to us about the trustworthiness of the Scriptures?*

      _____

      _____

      _____

      _____

      NOTES: The purification or smelting of silver is carried out in the following manner: the silver is liquefied in intense heat. At that point, the impurities float to the surface and are removed, leaving a purer form of silver. Going through this process "seven times" represents the absolute purity and trustworthiness of the Word of God.

2. Since the Scriptures alone are the infallible source of the knowledge of God and His will, what should be our response? What do the following texts teach us?

   a. *II Timothy 2:15*

_____

_____

_____

_____

_____

_____

   b. *Ezra 7:10*

_____

_____

_____

_____

_____

_____

NOTES: Ezra did what Paul later commanded all of us in II Timothy 2:15—he was diligent to study the Scriptures. Notice the completeness of Ezra's response to God's Word: (1) he studied the Scriptures; (2) he practiced or obeyed the Scriptures; and (3) he taught others the Scriptures. We should do the same!

3. We mentioned above that we should seek the knowledge of God not only through the careful study of the Scriptures but also through prayer. Prayer is an essential element to all that we do in the Christian life, especially with regard to the knowledge of God and the study of

Scripture. Below are two examples of crying out to God for greater knowledge of His person and will. What do they promise? How can they be applied to our own search for a greater knowledge of God?

a. *Psalm 119:18*

_____

_____

_____

_____

_____

b. *Jeremiah 33:2-3*

_____

_____

_____

_____

_____

Chapter 3: God Is One and Three

GOD IS ONE

It is the testimony of the Scriptures that there is only one true God. The belief in one God is termed "monotheism" [Greek: **mónos** = one, alone + **theós** = god], while the belief in more than one god is called "polytheism" [Greek: **polús** or **polýs** = much, many + **theós** = god]. The Christian faith is **monotheistic**.

1. In Deuteronomy 6:4 is found one of the most important declarations in all the Scriptures. What does this declaration affirm?

    _____

    _____

    _____

    _____

    _____

    _____

NOTES: There is only one true God. This is the foundation stone of the Old Testament and New Testament faith. It is important to understand that the word "one" comes from the Hebrew word **echad**, which often refers to a unity of more than one person. For example, in Genesis 2:24 we read, "…they (*i.e.* the man and the woman) shall become **one** flesh"; and in Ezra 3:1, "…the people gathered together as **one** man." This truth will have great importance in the next section, where we will explore what it means that the one true God exists as a Trinity: the Father, Son, and Holy Spirit.

2. What do the following Scriptures affirm about the nature of God? Are there any other gods apart from the God of the Scriptures? Explain your answer.

    a. *Deuteronomy 4:39*

    _____

    _____

_____

_____

_____

NOTES: The belief in the one true and living God of the Scriptures must be firmly rooted in the deepest part of our heart and mind. It is the foundation stone of the rest of our faith. Also, it is important to recognize that the God of the Scriptures is not just a god of a certain location or realm (as many pagan deities were thought to be). "Heaven and earth" represent the entire universe, both material and spiritual.

b. *Isaiah 43:10*

_____

_____

_____

_____

NOTES: Three important words are found in this text that direct us in our relationship with God. (1) **_Know_** – this denotes more than mere knowledge of God; it involves a personal relationship with Him. (2) **_Believe_** – our relationship with God requires not only knowledge but also trust or faith. (3) **_Understand_** – having believed in the one true God, we must seek to understand the implications. How then shall we live?

c. *Isaiah 45:18*

_____

_____

_____

_____

3. According to the following Scriptures, how should all men live in light of the truth that the God of the Bible is the one true and living God?

a. *Exodus 20:2-6*

_____

_____

_____

_____

_____

NOTES: The phrase "before Me" (v.3) is literally, "before My face." It means that the Lord should be our God and that there should be no other competing loyalties in our heart. Any person or thing that we value or serve more than God is a false god. The jealousy of God (v.5) should not be confused with the jealousy of sinful men that is a result of their envy and selfishness. God is jealous in that He will not surrender His claim to that which is rightfully His. He cannot deny who He is—the one true God, Creator of the heavens and the earth.

b. *Mark 12:28-30*

_____

_____

_____

_____

GOD IS A TRINITY

The word "trinity" comes from the Latin word **trinitas**, which means, "threefold" or "three in one." The Bible affirms that the one true God exists as a Trinity: the Father, Son, and Holy Spirit. They are three distinct Persons who are distinguishable from one another, and yet They share the same divine nature or **essence** and relate to one another in unbroken fellowship. It is important to note that the word "trinity" is not found in the Scriptures, but was first employed by Tertullian (one of the early Church Fathers) to describe what the Bible teaches about the triune nature of God.

1. In Matthew 28:19 is found the declaration used in every Christian baptism as commanded by the Lord Jesus Christ Himself. This declaration is a wonderful example of the unity and trinity of God.

    a. *The Lord Jesus commanded us to baptize in the N_____ of the Father, Son, and Holy Spirit.*

        NOTES: Notice that "name" is singular, and yet it is ascribed to three different Persons. The verse does not say in the **names** of the Father, Son, and Spirit, but in Their one **name**, because the Three are one.

2. The Trinitarian view of God that we discovered in Matthew 28:19 is seen throughout Scripture. Read II Corinthians 13:14, and then complete the phrases.

    a. *The grace of the Lord J_____ C_____.*

    b. *The love of G_____.*

    c. *And the fellowship of the H_____ S_____ be with you all.*

        NOTES: The above literary structure denotes absolute equality. It is noteworthy that the Son is mentioned even before the Father. It would be blasphemous to mention the Son and the Spirit in the same breath as God the Father if They were not equal with Him (see also I Corinthians 12:4-6; Ephesians 4:4-6; I Peter 1:2).

3. The Father, Son, and Holy Spirit are of one divine essence and dwell in perfect equality and unity; but They are also three distinct Persons, not simply one Person who reveals Himself in three different ways. In the following Scriptures, this truth is clearly affirmed. Fill in the blanks.

    a. *Mark 1:10-11*

        (1) The S_____ is baptized (v.10).

        (2) The S_____ descends (v.10).

        (3) The F_____ speaks from heaven (v.11).

    b. *John 14:16-17*

        (1) The S_____ prays to the Father (v.16).

        (2) The F_____ gives the Helper or Holy Spirit (vv.16-17).

        (3) The S_____ lives with and in the Christian (v.17).

        NOTES: From these simple texts of Scripture it is clear that the Father, Son, and Holy Spirit are three distinct Persons. God is not three independent Beings or three different Gods; nor is God one Person who wears three different masks or simply reveals Himself in three different forms. The God of the Scriptures exists as three distinct but equal Persons who are one in Their divine nature or essence and who dwell in perfect equality and unity.

4. Although the Father, Son, and Holy Spirit are equal and exist in perfect unity, They often carry out distinct functions and manifest Themselves in different ways. What do the following Scriptures teach us about this truth? Fill in the blanks with the correct answer found in each Scripture.

   a. *The F_____ is the invisible God who no man has seen (John 1:18).*

   b. *The S_____ is God made flesh and the perfect revelation of the Father (John 1:1,14, 18; 14:9).*

   c. *The S_____ is God living in the Christian (Romans 8:9; John 14:16-17, 23).*

SUMMARY TRUTHS ABOUT THE TRINITY

From the Scriptures we have studied in this chapter, we may affirm the following truths about God.

1. **God is One.** There are not three different Gods in the Trinity—a heresy called "tritheism."

2. **God is Three.** There is one God who exists as three Persons: the Father, the Son, and the Holy Spirit.

3. **The Scriptures clearly affirm both of these important truths: God is One, and God is Three.** Although we cannot fully comprehend how this can be, we must believe and teach both truths with equal conviction. Heresy (*i.e.* false doctrine) occurs when we affirm one truth and deny the other, or emphasize one truth over the other. We must hold to all truth equally and avoid all extremes.

4. **The three Persons of the Trinity are real and distinct Persons.** The Trinity is not just one Person who wears three different masks or who reveals Himself in three different forms or modes—a heresy called "modalism."

5. **The three Persons of the Trinity are perfectly equal.** The Son is not less than the Father, nor is the Spirit less than the Son.

6. **The three Persons of the Trinity may manifest Themselves in different ways and may carry out different functions.** No man has seen the Father; the Son became flesh and dwelled among men; the Spirit dwells within every believer in Christ.

7. **The mystery of the Trinity is not grounds for its denial.** Some may say that they cannot believe what they cannot understand—if something cannot be explained, it cannot be true. If we were to apply this same logic to the entire Bible or even to our own existence, then there would be very little left for us to believe. Even the simplest truths of Scripture and of human reality go beyond our understanding. Our belief is based not upon our understanding but upon the true testimony of the Holy Scriptures.

8. **Most illustrations used to explain the Trinity are woefully inadequate.** Often, students of the Bible have resorted to various illustrations in an attempt to explain the Trinity. Regretfully, these illustrations often do more harm than good. For example, the Trinity is sometimes compared to water, which commonly exists in three different forms—liquid, ice, and steam. Such an illustration is a distortion of the Trinity in that it suggests (as in modalism above) that God is one Person who takes three different forms. It is better to simply affirm both the oneness and threeness of God without explanation or illustration than to give an explanation or illustration that is misleading or even heretical.

IMPLICATIONS OF THE TRINITY

The doctrine of the Trinity is not mere theological speculation but the clear teaching of the Scriptures. However, it is not enough that we affirm the Trinity as biblical; we must also understand something of its implications. In the following, we will mention some of the most obvious and important ones.

1. **The Trinity teaches us that God is relational**. The Father, Son, and Spirit have existed together throughout eternity in a mutual relationship of perfect unity and love. The believer has been invited to enter into this fellowship (John 14:16, 23).

2. **The Trinity teaches us that God has no need.** God did not make man or redeem a people for Himself because He was lonely or needy, but for His own glory, and out of His superabundance. The three Persons of the Trinity are perfectly satisfied in one another. God has no need to be made complete by anything or anyone outside of Himself.

3. **The Trinity teaches us that God is love.** Love is not just an action, but also an attribute of God. This attribute is eternal. It is not something that began with creation. Long before the universe was made, God was love, and a perfect expression of this love was found among the Persons of the Trinity.

4. **The Trinity teaches us that our salvation is the work of God.** The Father, who designed our salvation and governs its every detail, is God. The Son, upon whose person and work our salvation depends, is God. The Spirit, who indwells us and seals us for the day of redemption, is God (Ephesians 4:30). Each Person involved in our salvation is fully God. Therefore, we can have unwavering confidence that the God who began a good work in us will finish it without fail (Philippians 1:6).

5. **The Trinity is a model for our human relationships.** The three Persons of the Trinity dwell together in pure equality and unity, yet have different roles or functions. This is especially evident in the Son's submission to the Father. Although equal with the Father, He submitted to the Father's will and humbled Himself by becoming obedient to the point of death (Philippians 2:6-8). This proves that submission in its proper context is not demeaning to the individual's dignity or a mark of inferiority. This has special application for each aspect of human relationships, especially with regard to church life (leaders and the congregation), marriage (husbands and wives), family (parents and children), and employment (employers and employees).

Chapter 4: The Deity of the Son and the Spirit

The word "deity" comes from the Latin word **deitas**, which denotes divinity or the state of being God. The deity of the Son and the Spirit are two of the most important doctrines in Christianity. A person simply cannot be a Christian without recognizing that the Son and the Spirit are God, the second and third Persons of the Trinity—the Son, who became flesh for our salvation, and the Spirit, who indwells every believer.

The truth of the Father's deity is rarely disputed. Even many of the sects that deny the deity of the Son and the Spirit affirm that the Father is God (I Corinthians 8:6). For this reason, there is no need for us to consider the many texts that affirm His deity. On the other hand, the deity of the Son and the deity of the Spirit have been under constant attack throughout the near two thousand years of Christian history. Therefore, it is absolutely essential that every true follower of Christ learn from the Scriptures that both the Son and the Spirit are fully divine in the strictest sense of the term.

THE SON IS GOD

1. In John 1:1 is found one of the most important texts in the Scriptures regarding the deity of the Son of God. Read the text carefully, and then complete the following exercise.

   a. *In the B_____*. This is a reference to the beginning of creation (Genesis 1:1).

   b. *Was the W_____*. This is translated from the Greek word **lógos**. In Greek philosophy, it referred to an impersonal force or reason that gave unity and order to the universe. In the Old Testament, it referred to the communication or self-expression of God. God created all things through the Word (Genesis 1:3, 9), and He reveals Himself to men through the Word. John does not identify the "Word" until verse 14. There we see that the "Word" is the Son, who became flesh and dwelled among us. The Apostle Paul writes that the Son existed before all things (Colossians 1:17) and that God created all things through Him (verse 16). The Apostle John writes that it is through the Son that God has explained Himself or made Himself known (John 1:18).

   c. *And the Word was W_____ God.* Here we learn two great truths: (1) the Son is a Person distinct from God the Father; and (2) the Son existed in perfect fellowship with God the Father before anything was made.

   d. *And the Word was G_____*. It would be difficult, if not impossible, for John to make a clearer declaration regarding the deity of the Son. Some sects teach that the Son is being referred to as "a god" instead of "the God," because there is no definite article before the word "god" in the original language of the New Testament (Greek: **theós**). Their argument is refuted on two grounds. First, in John 1:6, 12, 13, and 18 the Greek word **theós** (God) is used without a definite article and yet clearly refers to God.

The meaning of a term is always determined by its context. Secondly, to say that the Son is "a god" contradicts all the other Scriptures that declare that there is no other god of any kind (Isaiah 44:6, 8; 45:5, 21; 64:4; I Corinthians 8:4).

2. John 1:18 is another important text regarding the deity of the Son. Read the text, and carefully consider its truths. Then complete the following exercise by filling in the blanks.

   a. *No one has seen G_____ at any time.* This is a clear reference to God the Father, who dwells in unapproachable light (I Timothy 6:16). All visions of God in the Old Testament were only very limited revelations. No one has seen or can see God in the fullness of His glory (I Timothy 6:16).

   b. *The only B_____ G_____.* The phrase "only begotten" would be better translated, "only" or "one and only." The Greek term is **monogenês [mónos** = one, alone + **génos** = kind or species], which denotes uniqueness or the "one-of-a-kind" nature of something. It does not mean that the Son was born or begotten, but that He is the "one and only." The word "Son" is found in some translations in the place of the word "God." This is due to the fact that both words are found in different ancient Greek manuscripts. However, the word "God" has the strongest support. Other translations: "No one has ever seen God; the only God, who is at the Father's side, he has made him known" (ESV). "No one has ever seen God. The only one, himself God, who is in closest fellowship with the Father, has made God known" (NET).

   c. *Who is in the B_____ of the F_____.* This is an even more beautiful description of the truth revealed in John 1:1—"the Word was **with** God." The Son always dwells in the most perfect fellowship of intimacy and love with the Father and the Spirit. The uniqueness of the Son is revealed in that He has a one-of-a-kind relationship with God the Father.

   d. *He has E_____ Him.* Only God can fully comprehend God or fully make Him known. Only in the Son does the fullness of God dwell (Colossians 1:19). He alone is the image of the invisible God (Colossians 1:15), and He alone is able to communicate Him to man.

3. What does Philippians 2:6 teach about the Son of God prior to Him taking on flesh and becoming man?

   _____

   _____

   _____

   _____

NOTES: The word "form" comes from the Greek word **morphê**, which refers not only to the outward or external appearance of something or someone, but also to its essential character or underlying reality. The Son did not just "seem" to be God in appearance, but "was" God in reality. The word "equal" comes from the Greek word *ísos*, which means, "to be equal in quantity or quality." This is an unmistakable reference to the deity of Christ. He existed throughout all eternity, bearing the form of God and being equal with God in every way. Even when He emptied Himself and became a man, He did not cease to be God (verse 7). He emptied Himself of the privileges of deity, but not of deity itself.

4. What does Colossians 1:15 teach us about the deity of the Son of God and His exalted rank above all creation?

_____

_____

_____

_____

NOTES: The word "image" comes from the Greek word *eikôn*, which is properly translated, "image" or "likeness." Who but God could be the exact image of God? Any lesser being would not be a true image of God's infinite excellencies, but only a slight and distorted misrepresentation. The Son can be the image of God only because "He is the radiance of His glory and the exact representation of His nature" (Hebrews 1:3). The word "firstborn" comes from the Greek word *prōtotókos* [*prôtos* = first + *tíktō* = to bring forth] and has often been used erroneously to deny the deity of Christ. The apostle did not use this term to show that the Son was a creature, but rather to prove that He held a rank far above all creation and was distinct from it. The true meaning of "firstborn" with regard to the Son is clearly illustrated in Psalm 89:27, where the term is used to show rank rather than origin or birth. In reference to David, God declares, "I also shall make him my firstborn, the highest of the kings of the earth." It is clear that David was the "firstborn" of God only in the sense that he was ranked above all other kings. In a similar (yet more far-reaching) manner, the Son of God is "firstborn" in the sense that He is over all creation.

5. In Colossians 1:19, we find still another affirmation of the Son's deity. What great truths are communicated, and how do they demonstrate that the Son is God?

_____

_____

_____

NOTES: The fullness of the ocean cannot be contained in a cup that can be held in a man's hand. Neither would it be possible for the fullness of God to dwell in any being less than God.

6. We will conclude this section with a consideration of a few more important texts in which the Son is referred to directly as God. It is important to note that these references with regard to the Son's deity were made even after His incarnation. The truth communicated is that when the eternal Son became a man, He did not cease to be God in any sense of the term.

   a. *My L_____ and my G_____ (John 20:28).* The first title comes from the Greek word **kúrios**, which is used throughout the Septuagint (Greek Old Testament) as a reference to Yahweh (or Jehovah). The second title comes from the Greek word for God—**theós**. If Thomas's words had been the result of misdirected zeal, Jesus would have surely corrected him. If Jesus were not Lord and God, both Thomas and Jesus would be equally guilty of blasphemy—the worst of all possible offenses against God.

   b. *Our great G_____ and S_____ (Titus 2:13).* This is yet another direct reference to the Son as God. However, we must not overlook that the title of "Savior" is also a great proof of the Son's deity. In Isaiah 43:10-11, God declares, "I, even I, am the LORD, and there is no savior besides Me." If Christ is our Savior, then He is also God. If He is not God, then He cannot be our Savior. Regarding the Son, Peter says, "There is salvation in no one else" (Acts 4:12). Therefore, He must be God!

   c. *The One who is over all, G_____ blessed forever (Romans 9:5).* Having affirmed the incarnation of the Son ("Christ according to the flesh"), Paul then affirms that He is God. The phrase may also be translated, "who is God over all, blessed forever" (ESV/NET).

   d. *Your T_____, O G_____ (Hebrews 1:8).* In this context, the Father Himself refers to His Son as God. After His death and resurrection, the Son of God was once again exalted to the right hand of His Father, where He reigns as God and Man.

THE SPIRIT IS GOD

1. In Acts 5:3-4, the Apostle Peter confronts Ananias about his and his wife's greed and deception. In doing so, he also provides us with insight into the nature and deity of the Spirit. Read the text until you understand its contents, and then fill in the blanks.

   a. *According to verse 3, Peter declared that Ananias had lied to the H_____*

   S_____.

   b. *According to verse 4, Peter declared that Ananias had lied to G_____.*

   NOTES: This is a strong affirmation not only of the Spirit's deity but also of the truth that the Spirit is a Person and not an impersonal power. To lie to the Holy Spirit is to lie to God because the Spirit is God.

2. In I Corinthians 3:16 and 6:19, the Apostle Paul teaches us that the believer is the temple of God. In doing so, he also provides us with even greater understanding about the deity of the Spirit. Read both texts, and then complete the following exercise.

a. *In I Corinthians 3:16, the believer is called the temple of G_____.*

b. *In I Corinthians 6:19, the believer is called the temple of the H_____*

   S_____.

   NOTES: In these two texts, we have a powerful affirmation of the Spirit's deity. In I Corinthians 3:16, the believer is called the temple of God, but in I Corinthians 6:19, the believer is referred to as the temple of the Holy Spirit. To use these two terms interchangeably would be unthinkable to the Apostle Paul if he did not view the Spirit as fully God and a real Person of the Trinity.

3. In Romans 8:9 is found not only a declaration of the Spirit's deity but also a beautiful and powerful picture of the Trinity. Fill in the blanks with the references to the Holy Spirit in this verse.

a. *The S_____. The Holy Spirit is a real Person, distinct from the Father and the Son.*

b. *The S_____ of G_____. God the Father and the Holy Spirit are one.*

c. *The S_____ of C_____. God the Son and the Holy Spirit are one.*

Chapter 5: God Is Spirit

God is not material or corporeal (*i.e.* He does not possess a physical body). Two of the greatest implications of this truth are: (1) God is not confined to any of the physical restraints so common to humanity; and (2) God is not visible and should therefore never be degraded with images made by men. At times, the Scriptures speak of God as if He possessed a physical body. There are references to His arms, back, breath, ears, eyes, face, feet, fingers, and more. How do we explain these references in light of the truth that God is spirit? In theology, these references are considered **anthropomorphic** [Greek: **ánthrōpos** = man + **morphê** = form] expressions. In other words, God is simply attributing to Himself human characteristics in order to communicate a truth about Himself in a way that men can comprehend. For example, the Bible speaks of God's "wings" and of His people "hiding under the shadow of His wings" (Exodus 19:4; Ruth 2:12; Psalm 17:8; 36:7; 57:1; 61:4; 63:7; 91:4). It would be absurd to interpret such statements literally.

1. How do the Scriptures describe God in John 4:24?

   a. *God is S_____.*

   b. *Based upon the explanation given in the introductory paragraph, write a brief summary of the meaning of the statement, "God is spirit."*

   _____

   _____

   _____

   _____

   _____

2. How should we live in light of the truth that God is spirit? Write your thoughts about the following truths based upon the associated Scriptures.

   a. *We must worship God sincerely (John 4:24).*

   _____

   _____

   _____

_____

_____

NOTES: The reference to worshiping God "in spirit" has two possible meanings: (1) we must worship God with all our being, sincerely and profoundly; or (2) we must worship God in the power and under the direction of the Holy Spirit. The reference to worshiping God "in truth" also has two possible meanings: (1) we must worship God truthfully, sincerely, and with integrity; or (2) we must worship God according to the truth—*i.e.* according to the will of God revealed in the Scriptures.

b. *We must avoid associating God with a religious building or ascribing to God any human limitation or need (Acts 17:24-25).*

_____

_____

_____

_____

_____

NOTES: The fact that God has no need is wonderfully demonstrated in Psalm 50:10-12—"For every beast of the forest is Mine, the cattle on a thousand hills. I know every bird of the mountains, and everything that moves in the field is Mine. If I were hungry I would not tell you, for the world is Mine, and all it contains."

3. How do the Scriptures describe God in Hebrews 11:27?

a. *God is He who is U_____.*

NOTES: If God is invisible, how do we explain the passages of Scripture where He seems to reveal Himself in a visible form? To answer, we must first understand two principles of Bible interpretation. First, the Bible does not contradict itself. Second, the passages of Scripture that are difficult to interpret with certainty should be interpreted in light of those passages whose interpretation is unmistakable. The Scriptures clearly state that God is invisible; therefore, the "visible" appearances of God in the Scriptures (with the exception of the incarnation of the Son of God) should be interpreted as "visions"—symbolic representations of spiritual reality. Ezekiel tells us (1:1) that "the heavens were opened" and he "saw **visions** of God." In verse 28, the prophet summarizes these **visions** as "the appearance of the likeness of the glory of the Lord." In Daniel 7:9-15, Daniel sees a symbolic **vision** of God the Father as the "Ancient of Days." In Luke 3:22, John the Baptist sees a **vision** of the heavens "opening" and the Holy Spirit descending with the appearance of a dove (the symbolism is obvious).

4. What do the following Scriptures affirm about God, especially about His invisibility?

   a. *I Timothy 1:17*

   _____

   _____

   _____

   b. *I Timothy 6:15-16*

   _____

   _____

   _____

   NOTES: God's invisibility is mentioned as one of the attributes that distinguishes Him from His creation. God's person and existence are unfathomable. He can only be known to the degree that He chooses to reveal Himself.

5. According to the following texts, how should we live in light of the truth of God's invisibility?

   a. *Deuteronomy 4:11-12; 15-16*

   _____

   _____

   _____

NOTES: Any attempt to make a figure or drawing of the living God will lead to a distortion of His image and a diminishing of His glory. Therefore, all forms of idolatry must be avoided like the plague. Furthermore, we must seek to think only those thoughts about God that are firmly grounded and supported by the Scriptures.

b. *I Timothy 1:17; 6:15-16*

_____

_____

_____

_____

6. God is immaterial (*i.e.* spirit) and invisible. How then can we know such a God? According to the following Scriptures, how has God revealed Himself (*i.e.* made Himself known) to men?

a. *According to the words of Jesus in John 6:46, has any man ever seen the Father? Who has seen the Father?*

_____

_____

_____

_____

b. *If no one has ever seen God the Father except for the Son, how has the Father made Himself known to men? How can we understand who God is? Who can explain such things to us? What does John 1:18 teach us?*

_____

_____

_____

_____

NOTES: The word "explained" comes from the Greek word *exēgéomai*, which means, "to interpret, explain, exposit, or expound." The Son explains God to us through His life and His teaching. The NET Bible provides us with a very useful translation: "No one has ever seen God. The only one, himself God, who is in closest fellowship with the Father, has made God known."

c. *According to the following Scriptures, why is Jesus uniquely qualified to show us God the Father?*

(1) Colossians 1:15; Hebrews 1:3

_____

_____

_____

_____

NOTES: The word "image" comes from the Greek word *eikôn*, which is properly translated, "image" or "likeness." Who but God could be the exact image of God? Any lesser being would not be a true image of God's infinite excellencies, but only a slight and distorted representation. The Son can be the image of God only because "He is the radiance of His glory and the exact representation of His nature" (Hebrews 1:3).

(2) John 14:9

_____

_____

_____

_____

NOTES: It is important to recognize that Jesus' words would be blasphemy if He were not God in the fullest and strictest sense of the term. It is a foundational truth of Christianity that everything that we might ever want to discover about God is found in the Man Christ Jesus.

Chapter 6: God Is Personal

One of the most important truths of Scripture is that God is not an impersonal force, thoughtlessly moving the universe; nor is He a capricious power, coldly manipulating His creation for some selfish end. The Scriptures teach us that God is personal (*i.e.* He possesses a distinguishable personality); He is aware of His own existence, has both an intellect and a will, and is capable of entering into a personal relationship with man.

GOD IS AWARE OF HIS OWN EXISTENCE

It may seem unnecessary to say that God is aware of His own existence, but this is one of the most fundamental characteristics of one who has a personality. There are many religions outside of Christianity whose concept of "god" is that of either an impersonal force (Buddhism, Taoism, etc.) or an essence that dwells within all things (pantheism [Greek: ***pás*** = all + ***theós*** = god]). In contrast, the God of the Scriptures is a personal Being who is aware of His own existence as distinct from all other beings and things.

1. That God is aware of His own existence is clearly revealed in the Scriptures. How does God refer to Himself in Exodus 3:14?

   a. *I A_____.*

      NOTES: This declaration is a powerful affirmation that God recognizes His own existence. He knows that He is and that He is distinct from all created persons and things.

2. The Scriptures teach us not only that God is aware of His own existence, but also that He is aware of His individuality (*i.e.* His distinctness from all created persons and things). According to the Scriptures, what does God declare about His own unique existence apart from anyone or anything else?

   a. *There is no O_____ God besides Him (Isaiah 45:21).*

   b. *There is none E_____ Him (Isaiah 45:21).*

   c. *There is none to whom we may L_____ (or compare) Him (Isaiah 40:25).*

   d. *There is none that is His E_____ (Isaiah 40:25).*

      NOTES: Each one of these declarations proves that God is both distinct and independent from all other individuals and things.

GOD POSSESSES AN INTELLECT

The intellect is considered to be one of the primary characteristics of personhood. The word comes from the Latin word **intellegere** [**inter** = between or among + **legere** = to pick or choose] and refers to the ability to reason, perceive, or understand. According to the Scriptures, God possesses an intellect that goes far beyond human comprehension. Nothing is beyond His knowledge or understanding.

1. What do the following Scriptures teach us about God's intellect?

    a. *Psalm 92:5*

    _____

    _____

    _____

    _____

    b. *Romans 11:33-36*

    _____

    _____

    _____

    _____

2. In the following Scriptures, how is man's intellect or understanding described in comparison with that of God?

    a. *Psalm 94:11; I Corinthians 3:20*

    _____

    _____

    _____

    _____

b. *Isaiah 55:8-9*

_____

_____

_____

_____

c. *I Corinthians 1:20, 25*

_____

_____

_____

_____

3. God's knowledge and understanding are far beyond the comprehension of finite men. According to the following Scriptures, how may man come to understand (at least, in part) the infinite things of God?

a. *Through the Son of God (John 1:18)*

_____

_____

_____

_____

b. *Through the Spirit of God (I Corinthians 2:11-12)*

_____

_____

_____

_____

_____

NOTES: This text refers to the believer's relationship with the Holy Spirit. The primary means by which the Spirit teaches God's people is by illuminating the truths of the Scriptures.

    c. *Through the Word of God (Psalm 119:97-100)*

_____

_____

_____

_____

_____

4. In Deuteronomy 29:29, the Scriptures declare: "The secret things belong to the LORD our God, but the things revealed belong to us..." According to Psalm 131:1-3, how should we live (*i.e.* what should be our attitude) in light of the infinite knowledge of God?

_____

_____

_____

_____

_____

GOD POSSESSES A WILL

The Scriptures clearly reveal that God possesses a will—the power to determine His actions (*i.e.* what He will do) and the end or purpose of His creation (*i.e.* He can do what He wills with what He has made). God's choices flow from who He is; His will is an expression of His being and disposition. It is important to understand that the will of God and the will of man are two very different things. God is the only One who is completely free to do whatever He purposes in Himself, without limitations or the possibility of failure. The most resolute decisions of the most powerful men often come to nothing.

1. What do the following Scriptures teach us about the will of God? Are there any limitations to the will of God? Can any power thwart the will of God?

   a. *Proverbs 19:21*

   b. *Isaiah 14:27*

   c. *Isaiah 46:9-10*

   d. *Daniel 4:34-35*

e. *Ephesians 1:11*

_____

_____

_____

_____

_____

2. Although God's will cannot be limited by any person or force outside of Himself, there are some things that God will not do simply because they contradict His most holy and righteous character. According to the following Scriptures, what are some things that God will not do? How is this truth a comfort and a blessing to us?

a. *Titus 1:2*

_____

_____

_____

_____

_____

b. *II Timothy 2:13*

_____

_____

_____

_____

_____

c. *James 1:13*

_____

_____

_____

_____

_____

_____

NOTES: There are two great truths communicated in this text. First, God cannot be tempted, because He is morally perfect and every form of evil is repulsive to Him. Secondly, God does not tempt anyone. He may test His people for their good, but He does not tempt them or entice them to sin.

Chapter 7: God Is Relational

It is the testimony of Scripture that God desires a personal relationship with His creation, especially with man, who has been created in His image (Genesis 1:27). This is one of the greatest truths of Christianity. God is not an impersonal "it," incapable of entering into a relationship with others; and man is not a cosmic accident, alone in the universe. God created man that man might know Him and be a recipient of His goodness. When man's relationship with God was broken through sin, God sent His own Son in order that the relationship might be restored. Those who have been reconciled with God through faith in His Son may have the greatest confidence that God seeks a personal, vital, and growing relationship with them.

1. From Genesis to Revelation, the Scriptures portray God as One who desires to enter into fellowship with His creation, especially with man, in spite of his sin. In a very real sense, the Bible is a record of God seeking sinful men and working to restore His relationship with them. This truth is clearly seen even in the fall of Adam and Eve.

   a. *According to Genesis 3:8-10, how did Adam's sin affect his attitude toward God?*

   _____

   _____

   _____

   _____

   b. *How did Adam's sin affect God's relationship with him (Genesis 3:23-24)?*

   _____

   _____

   _____

   _____

   NOTES: In Genesis 3:21-24, we discover both the judgment and the mercy of God toward sinful man. The judgment of God is seen in that He drove Adam and Eve from the garden, which represents the separation or broken fellowship that exists between

God and the sinner. The mercy of God is here revealed in two distinct ways. First, God barred Adam's way to the tree of life so that he would not eat of it and live forever in a state of sinful corruption and alienation from God (vv.22-24). Second, God took the life of an innocent victim to provide coverings for Adam and Eve (v.21). This represents the sacrifice of an innocent party in the place of the guilty and finds its ultimate fulfillment in the sacrifice of God's only Son on Calvary for the sins of the world.

2. How does Isaiah 59:1-2 explain the change in God's relationship with Adam? What does it teach us about our own sin and how it affects our relationship with God?

_____

_____

_____

_____

_____

NOTES: Here the intolerance of God toward sin is revealed. Because God is holy and righteous, outstanding sin will always lead to separation between God and the sinner. In Habakkuk 1:13, the prophet declared the following about the holiness of God and His relationship with sin: "Your eyes are too pure to approve evil, and You cannot look on wickedness with favor." It is for this reason that God sent His only Son to pay our sin debt that He might have unbroken fellowship with us through faith (Romans 5:1).

3. According to Genesis 3:8-9, who sought after Adam and Eve immediately after their fall? What does this teach us about God's character and His desire to have a relationship with fallen man?

_____

_____

_____

_____

4. According to Acts 17:26-27, why has God sovereignly determined the times and places in which all men are born and live? How does this demonstrate that God is relational and desires to have a relationship with fallen man?

_____

_____

_____

_____

5. According to Luke 19:10, why did God send His Son to earth? What was the purpose of His incarnation? How does this demonstrate that God is relational and desires to have a relationship with fallen man?

_____

_____

_____

_____

NOTES: It is important to note that this statement was made during Jesus' visit to the home of Zaccheus. He was a tax collector and a notorious sinner. By his own admission, he had defrauded others in order to enrich himself. Luke's account of this meeting between Jesus and Zaccheus simply illustrates the truth that Jesus declared in Luke 19:10—He had "come to seek and to save that which was lost."

6. According to the following Scriptures, what has the Son of God accomplished so that man's broken relationship with God might be restored?

   a. *Romans 5:8-10*

_____

_____

_____

_____

_____

_____

b. *Colossians 1:19-22*

_____

_____

_____

_____

_____

_____

7. According to John 17:3, what is the essence of eternal life? How does this demonstrate that God is relational and desires to have a relationship with His people?

_____

_____

_____

_____

NOTES: The word "know" means a great deal more than simply impersonal or factual knowledge. It denotes an intimate, personal relationship. Eternal life is much more than a life of infinite duration. It is a superior quality of life, marked by unbroken fellowship with God. This is one of God's great purposes for reconciling us to Himself through His Son.

8. As Christians, we have a restored relationship with God founded upon the perfect work of Christ on our behalf. It is a relationship that cannot be broken. This truth should cause us not

to be apathetic about sin, but to separate ourselves from anything that might be an obstacle to our fellowship with God. What do the following Scriptures teach us about this truth?

a. *II Corinthians 6:14-18*

_____

_____

_____

_____

_____

NOTES: This text is not teaching us to withdraw from all unbelievers. In Paul's first letter to the Corinthians he wrote: "I wrote you in my letter not to associate with immoral people; I did not at all mean with the immoral people of this world, or with the covetous and swindlers, or with idolaters, for then you would have to go out of the world" (I Corinthians 5:9-10). The idea in II Corinthians 6:14-18 is that we are to withdraw from anything that is directly prohibited in the Scriptures or that can lead us into sin.

b. *II Timothy 2:19*

_____

_____

_____

_____

_____

NOTES: The word "abstain" comes from the Greek word **aphístēmi**, which means, "to withdraw, remove, depart, or leave." We are called to abstain from wickedness and distance ourselves from it.

9. As we have already stated, the believer has a restored relationship with God that is founded upon the perfect work of Christ. However, this truth should not lead to apathy. It should result not only in our abstaining from sin, but also in our active pursuit of God to cultivate a deeper relationship with Him. What do the following Scriptures teach us about this truth?

a. *Hosea 6:3*

_____

_____

_____

_____

b. *Psalm 27:4*

_____

_____

_____

_____

c. *Psalm 27:8*

_____

_____

_____

_____

10. As Christians, we not only have the responsibility to watch over our relationship with God, but we also have the responsibility to announce the gospel to others so that they too might enter into the same restored relationship with God. What does II Corinthians 5:18-20 teach us about this truth?

_____

_____

_____

_____

Chapter 8: God Is Great

There is only one God, and He alone is great. All other beings and things are totally dependent upon His goodness and strength. A comparison should never be made between God and any other creature or thing. As the self-existent Creator, He is infinitely above His dependent and finite creation. The mightiest archangel is no closer to being like God than the tiniest microbe. God is incomparable! In the context of the body of believers, this truth is extremely important. There are no great men or women of God in the Scriptures or in Church history; there are only weak, sinful, and faithless men and women of a great and merciful God!

1. How is God described in the following Scriptures?

    a. *The Lord is a great G_____ and a great K_____* (Psalm 95:3).

    b. *The Lord is the G_____ and A_____ God (Daniel 9:4).*
        The word "awesome" comes from the Hebrew word **yare** which means, "to fear, revere, or be afraid." Even the smallest revelation of God's greatness and holiness would strike even the most splendid of His creatures with astonishment, reverence, and even fear. God is awesome; therefore, He is worthy of the greatest reverence.

    c. *The Lord is very G_____; He is clothed with splendor and majesty (Psalm 104:1).* God's splendor and majesty are not some external things that He puts on; they are a part of His very being. Unlike men, God has no need to add something to Himself in order to enhance His greatness or His beauty.

2. How is the greatness of God described in Psalm 145:3?

    a. *His greatness is U_____.*

        NOTES: God's greatness is beyond investigation or inquiry—it cannot be searched out or measured. It would be far easier to count the sand in all the oceans and deserts of the world or to number all the stars in the heavens than to measure the greatness of God.

3. What do the following Scriptures affirm about the greatness of God? How is the one true God contrasted with all other so-called gods?

    a. *Psalm 77:13*

    _____

    _____

    _____

b. *Psalm 86:10*

_____

_____

_____

_____

c. *Psalm 95:3*

_____

_____

_____

_____

d. *Psalm 135:5*

_____

_____

_____

_____

4. According to the following Scriptures, what should be our attitude and our response to the greatness of God? How should we live in light of His unsearchable greatness?

a. *Deuteronomy 32:3*

_____

_____

_____

_____

b. *I Chronicles 16:25*

_____

_____

_____

_____

c. *Psalm 104:1*

_____

_____

_____

_____

NOTES: The word "bless" comes from the Hebrew word **barak**. When directed toward God, it denotes a joyful exclamation of admiration, thanksgiving, and praise.

d. *Psalm 111:2*

_____

_____

_____

_____

e. *Psalm 138:5*

_____

_____

_____

_____

Chapter 9: God Is Perfect

The Scriptures teach us that God is perfect and lacks nothing in His person or works. There is no possibility of a defect in God. The perfection of God has some very important implications. First, it assures us that God will not change. He cannot become better than He is, because He is already perfect; and He cannot become less, because He would then cease to be God. Secondly, it assures us that God is worthy of our absolute trust.

THE WORKS OF GOD ARE PERFECT

God is perfect in every aspect of His character. The works of God, being an extension of His character, are also perfect. The implications of this truth are tremendous and should produce in us a confidence that will prevail against the greatest doubts. All that God has ever done or will ever do in the universe and in each of us is perfect.

1. What do the following Scriptures teach us about the perfection of God's works?

   a. *Deuteronomy 32:3-4*

   _____

   _____

   _____

   _____

   b. *Psalm 18:30*

   _____

   _____

   _____

   _____

NOTES: The word "blameless" comes from the Hebrew word **tamim**, which may also be translated, "perfect." It is important to note that there is a direct relationship between God's character, His works, and His Word. Because God's character is perfect, His ways and Word are also perfect.

c. *Ecclesiastes 3:14*

_____

_____

_____

_____

NOTES: The completeness or perfection of God's works should lead us to fear or reverence Him.

2. God works not only in His creation but also in His people. Every Christian is a work of God. What do the following Scriptures teach us about this truth?

a. *Ephesians 2:10*

_____

_____

_____

_____

b. *Philippians 2:13*

_____

_____

_____

_____

c. *Philippians 1:6*

_____

_____

_____

_____

_____

3. The God of all creation is working in the life of every Christian. His work is perfect and will be accomplished without fail. This truth goes beyond what the human mind can comprehend— the perfect God is doing a perfect work in us to make us perfect. According to the following Scriptures, how should we respond to this truth?

a. *Psalm 92:4*

_____

_____

_____

_____

b. *Psalm 107:22*

_____

_____

_____

_____

c. *Philippians 2:12-13*

_____

_____

_____

_____

NOTES: As believers, we are not to "work for" our salvation, but we are to "work out" our salvation. We are to live out our Christian lives with a biblical reverence and trust in God. The word "trembling" possibly denotes both the seriousness of the

Christian life and the need for humility that leads us to distrust our own power and wisdom and to live in dependence upon God.

THE WILL OF GOD IS PERFECT

The will of God is perfect because it is founded upon His perfect and most holy character. The implications of this truth are tremendous. God's purpose and plan for us is worthy of absolute trust. We should never lean upon our own understanding or seek to do that which is only right in our own eyes. Rather, we should trust in God and obey His Word, the Holy Scriptures.

1. How is the will of God described in Romans 12:2?

   a. G_____. The word comes from the Greek word **agathós** and refers to that which is good, profitable, or upright.

   b. A_____. The word comes from the Greek word **euárestos** and refers to that which is well-pleasing, approved, or acceptable.

   c. P_____. The word comes from the Greek word **téleios** and refers to that which is complete and lacking in nothing.

   d. *How should the description of God's will in Romans 12:2 motivate us to live a life of obedience to the will of God?*

   _____

   _____

   _____

   _____

2. The following Scriptures give us insight regarding how to respond appropriately to the good, acceptable, and pleasing will of God. Read the texts, and write your thoughts.

   a. *According to Matthew 6:9-10, how should we pray concerning the will of God?*

   _____

   _____

b. *According to the following Scriptures, how should we do the will of God?*

(1) Psalm 40:8

_____

_____

_____

_____

_____

(2) Ephesians 6:6

_____

_____

_____

_____

_____

NOTES: In the immediate context, Paul is writing about the service that Christian slaves should render to their masters. However, the truths have a wider application to every area of the believer's life.

c. *How does the life of the Lord Jesus Christ demonstrate a correct attitude and response to the will of God? How should we imitate Him?*

(1) John 4:32-34

_____

_____

_____

_____

(2) John 5:30

_____

_____

_____

_____

3. One of the most important truths in Christianity is that the will of God is revealed first and foremost through the Word of God (*i.e.* the Scriptures). Like the will of God, the Word of God is perfect, because God is its Author and its Preserver. What do the following Scriptures teach us with regard to this truth? How should we respond?

a. *Psalm 19:7*

_____

_____

_____

_____

NOTES: The word "perfect" is translated from the Hebrew word **tamim**, which denotes that which is perfect, complete, sound, or blameless. The word "sure" comes from the Hebrew word **aman**, which denotes that which is confirmed, reliable, and trustworthy.

b. *Psalm 12:6*

_____

_____

_____

_____

NOTES: The Scriptures are absolutely reliable as a means of knowing the will of God. The ancients had a very effective process for refining or purifying silver. It was melted down with intense heat. Then, the impurities would rise to the surface and be removed. To say that the Word of God is like silver refined seven times communicates its absolute purity and, by extension, its reliability.

c. *II Timothy 3:16-17*

_____

_____

_____

_____

NOTES: The word "inspired" comes from the Greek word ***theópneustos***, which is literally translated, "God-breathed." The Scriptures are an absolutely reliable witness to the will of God because they "proceed out of the mouth of God" (Deuteronomy 8:3; Matthew 4:4).

4. The Word of God is the primary means through which the will of God is revealed. According to the following Scriptures, what should be our attitude and response to this truth?

a. *Psalm 1:1-2*

_____

_____

_____

_____

b. *Psalm 119:47-48*

_____

_____

c. *Psalm 119:127-128*

d. *Ezra 7:10*

e. *II Timothy 2:15*

Chapter 10: God Is Eternal

One of the most amazing attributes of God (and one of the many that distinguish Him from all creation) is His eternal existence—He is without beginning and without end. There was never a time when He did not exist, and there will never be a time when His existence will cease. He is before all things and will remain after all things have passed away. The eternality of God does not just mean that He has always existed and will exist for an infinite number of years; it further indicates that He is timeless and ageless, always existing and never changing. No person or created thing shares this attribute with Him. We are for a moment, but God is forever. He made us, but no one made Him. We depend upon Him for our very existence, but He depends upon nothing and no one. Our earthly existence passes away like sand through an hourglass, but He remains. He was God, is God, and will be God forever.

1. In the Scriptures, a person's name has great significance in that it often reveals something about his or her character. What are the names given to God in the following Scriptures, and what do they teach us about His eternality?

   a. *I A_____ Who I A_____ (Exodus 3:14).* The idea that is communicated in this statement is that existence is an attribute of God's very nature. Unlike man, God does not will to exist or make an effort to exist. He simply is.

   b. *The E_____ God (Isaiah 40:28).* One who is "everlasting" will "last forever." When applied to God, the word refers not only to the future, but also to the past. He has always been, and He will always be.

   c. *The A_____ of D_____ (Daniel 7:9).* When used with reference to men, the word "ancient" usually denotes old age and weakness of mind and body. When used with reference to God, it denotes the grandeur, splendor, power, and wisdom of the One who was before the very foundations of the world and will continue to be when the world has passed away.

   d. *The A_____ and the O_____ (Revelation 1:8).* These are the first and last letters of the Greek alphabet. They powerfully communicate that God is the first and the last (see also Isaiah 44:6). He is before all things and will continue on when all things have passed.

2. Having considered the names of God that speak of His eternal nature, we will now consider some important declarations from Scripture. What do the following texts teach us about the eternal nature of God and His relationship to His creation? How do they demonstrate His greatness?

   a. *Job 36:26*

   _____

   _____

_____

_____

_____

b. *Psalm 90:2*

_____

_____

_____

_____

c. *Psalm 90:4; II Peter 3:8*

_____

_____

_____

_____

3. God is eternal, without beginning or end. What are the implications of His eternality for all of creation, especially for the people of God? What do the following Scriptures teach us? Write your thoughts.

   a. *God's Reign Is Eternal*

      (1) Jeremiah 10:10

      _____

      _____

      _____

(2) Psalm 45:6

_____

_____

_____

(3) Psalm 145:13; Daniel 4:34

_____

_____

_____

_____

b. *God's Word Is Eternal (Isaiah 40:6-8; see also I Peter 1:24-25)*

_____

_____

_____

_____

c. *God's Salvation and Care for His People Is Eternal*

(1) Deuteronomy 33:27

_____

_____

_____

NOTES: The phrase "dwelling place" refers to God as a refuge or hiding place for His people. The reference to God's arms "underneath" denotes the support and strength that He gives to His people.

(2) Psalm 48:14

_____

_____

_____

(3) Psalm 102:25-28

_____

_____

_____

_____

_____

NOTES: A contrast is drawn between the creation (_i.e._ heavens and the earth) and God's care for His people. The former is passing, but the latter is everlasting.

(4) Isaiah 26:3-4

_____

_____

_____

(5) Isaiah 40:28-31

_____

_____

_____

(6) Matthew 28:20

_____

_____

_____

_____

4. What should be our response to the truth of God's eternality? What should be our attitude, and how should we live before Him? What do the following Scriptures teach us?

   a. *I Chronicles 16:36*

   _____

   _____

   _____

   _____

   b. *Daniel 4:34*

   _____

   _____

   _____

   c. *I Timothy 1:17*

   _____

   _____

   _____

   _____

Chapter 11: God Is Self-Existent and Self-Sufficient

One of the most awe-inspiring and humbling truths about God is that He is absolutely free from any need or dependence. His existence, the fulfillment of His will, and His happiness or good pleasure do not depend upon anyone or anything outside of Himself. He is the only Being who is truly self-existent, self-sufficient, self-sustaining, independent, and free. All other beings derive their life and blessedness from God, but all that is necessary for God's existence and perfect happiness He finds in Himself. God has no lack or need and is dependent upon no one. To teach or even suggest that God made man because He was lonely or incomplete is a gross contradiction of the Scriptures. God did not create the universe or man because He had a need, but because He desired to make known the superabundance of His perfections, glory, and goodness.

1. In the Scriptures, a name has great significance in that it often reveals something about the one who bears it. What name does God ascribe to Himself in Exodus 3:14? What does it communicate to us about His self-sufficiency?

    a. *I A_____ Who I A_____ (Exodus 3:14).*

    NOTES: This name demonstrates that God's existence was not caused, nor does it depend upon anything or anyone outside of Himself. It is God's nature to exist, and so He simply *is* without effort. God has no need that must be met, no void that must be filled, and no purpose that requires the aid of another. In I Corinthians 15:10, the Apostle Paul declared that which is true of all men: "By the grace of God I am what I am." Only God is able to declare, "I AM WHO I AM" by virtue of His own perfections and power.

2. What do the following Scriptures teach us about the self-existence and self-sufficiency of God? How do such attributes demonstrate God's greatness?

    a. *Psalm 36:9*

    _____

    _____

    _____

    _____

    _____

b. *John 5:26*

_____

_____

_____

_____

_____

_____

NOTES: God's life or existence is not derived from anyone or anything outside of Himself. He is life. It is His very nature to exist. The existence of all other things—visible or invisible, animate or inanimate—depends upon Him. Only God is truly free of need or dependence.

3. The self-sufficiency of God demonstrates His infinite greatness and His exalted place above His creation. All things depend upon Him for their very existence, yet He depends upon no one. In Acts 17:22-31, we find the Apostle Paul's sermon to the Epicurean and Stoic philosophers on Mars Hill. In verses 24-25, he refutes their idolatrous views by making three very important declarations about the true and living God. What do these declarations teach us about the self-sufficiency of God and His relationship to His creation?

a. *God does not dwell in temples made with hands (v.24).*

_____

_____

_____

_____

_____

NOTES: In Isaiah 66:1-2, God declares, "'Heaven is My throne and the earth is My footstool. Where then is a house you could build for Me? And where is a place that I may rest? For My hand made all these things, thus all these things came into being,' declares the LORD." In I Kings 8:27, Solomon prayed, "But will God indeed dwell on the earth? Behold, heaven and the highest heaven cannot contain You, how much less this house which I have built!"

b. *God is not served by human hands (v.25).*

_____

_____

_____

_____

_____

c. *God does not need anything (v.25).*

_____

_____

_____

_____

_____

4. To conclude our study of God's self-existence and self-sufficiency, we will consider Psalm 50:8-15. What does this passage teach us about these attributes of God and about our relationship with Him? Does God need anything from us? What does God desire from His people?

_____

_____

_____

_____

_____

NOTES: God does not need our help or even our sacrifices. What God desires from His people is trust, thanksgiving, and obedience. In I Samuel 15:22, the prophet Samuel declared, "Has the LORD as much delight in burnt offerings and sacrifices as in obeying the voice of the LORD? Behold, to obey is better than sacrifice, and to heed than the fat of rams."

Chapter 12: God Is Immutable

The word "immutable" comes from the Latin word **immutabilis** [**in** or **im** = not + **mutabilis** = mutable or changing]. Other words such as "unchanging," "constant," and "faithful" are helpful in understanding this divine attribute. The immutability of God means that He never changes in His attributes or counsel. God does not grow, evolve, or improve; He is already perfect. He cannot diminish, deteriorate, or regress, for then He would no longer be God. Whatever God is, He has always been and always will be. He does not change His mind or overrule one decree with another. He does not make a promise and then change His vow. He does not threaten and then not fulfill. This is especially comforting since the possibility of an Almighty God suddenly becoming evil or suddenly changing His mind is utterly terrifying. The immutability of God is one of His most important attributes because it guarantees that He and His Word will be the same yesterday, today, and forever (Hebrews 13:8). He is the only constant in the universe—the only One worthy of absolute trust.

1. In the Scriptures, a person's name has great significance in that it often describes who he is and reveals something about his character. What are the names given to God in the following Scriptures, and what do they teach us about His immutability?

   a. *I A_____ Who I A_____ (Exodus 3:14).* This name is derived from the Hebrew verb **hayah**, which means, "to be" or "to exist." It points not only to God's eternal nature and self-existence but also to His immutability. He **always is**, and He **always is the same**.

   b. *The R_____ (Deuteronomy 32:4).* This name needs little explanation. Within creation there are few things more permanent or unchanging than stone and rock and the mountains they form. It is a comfort to know that even this metaphor is inadequate. When all the rocks of this earth have turned to dust, God will remain unchanged.

2. Having considered the names of God that communicate His immutability, we will now turn to some of the most important biblical declarations regarding this attribute. What do they teach us about the unchanging nature of God and His relationship to His creation? How do they demonstrate His greatness?

   a. *Psalm 102:25-27*

   _____

   _____

   _____

   _____

_____

_____

b. *Malachi 3:6*

_____

_____

_____

_____

NOTES: This is a powerful demonstration of how God's immutability affects His relationship with His people. Even in the midst of Israel's unfaithfulness to God, He remained faithful, because He does not change and His promises do not fail.

c. *James 1:17*

_____

_____

_____

_____

NOTES: The New English Translation reads, "All generous giving and every perfect gift is from above, coming down from the Father of lights, with whom there is no variation or the slightest hint of change."

d. *Hebrews 13:8*

_____

_____

_____

_____

NOTES: Our salvation is secure because our Great God and Savior Jesus Christ (Titus 2:13) is immutable. His perfect character, the redemption He provided, and all His promises are the same yesterday, today, and forever.

3. Having considered many Scriptures that speak of the immutability of God's nature, we will now consider those passages that specifically speak of the immutability of His Word and counsel. What do the following Scriptures teach us about their unchanging nature? What do they teach us about God's relationship to His creation—especially to man?

   a. *I Samuel 15:29*

   _____

   _____

   _____

   _____

NOTES: This verse declares that God "is not man that He should change His mind." From this passage and others, it is clear that God's immutability extends even to His counsel and will. He is perfect in wisdom and therefore does not err in what He decrees; He is all-powerful and is therefore able to do all He has decided. But how do we reconcile this teaching with other Scriptures that seem to teach the contrary? In Genesis 6:6, God "was sorry that He had made man." In Exodus 32:9-14, the Lord "changed His mind" about destroying the disobedient nation of Israel. Finally, in Jonah 3:10, God "relented" concerning the calamity which He had declared He would bring upon the city of Nineveh. Do the Scriptures contradict themselves? Does God indeed change His mind? The answer is not as complex or mysterious as one might think. The Scriptures clearly teach that God's perfections, purposes, and promises are always the same. But this does not mean that His relationship with and disposition toward His ***ever-changing*** creation cannot vary. Genesis 6:6 simply refers to God's holy response to man's sin and His determination to blot out man from the face of the earth—v.7 (the same in I Samuel 15:11, 26). In Exodus 32:9-14, God "changed His mind" with regard to Israel's destruction as a gracious answer to Moses' prayer (a prayer that God led and empowered Moses to pray). In Jonah 3:4-10, God simply "relented" from destroying Nineveh when Nineveh "relented" from its sin. These passages are reminders to us that the ***immutability*** of God does not equate to ***immobility***. He does not change; but He is not static, apathetic, and uninvolved with His creation. He is dynamic, and He interacts with His creation. He is always the same, but His relationship and dealings with mutable men will vary according to how they respond to Him (Jeremiah 18:7-10; Ezekiel 18:21-24). This is not a contradiction to His immutability, but proof of it! He will always respond to men's actions in a manner consistent with His unchanging attributes.

b. *Numbers 23:19*

_____

_____

_____

_____

c. *Psalm 33:11*

_____

_____

_____

_____

4. It is important to understand that God's immutability depends not only upon His perfection but also upon His power. God would not be immutable if there existed some being or power greater than Him that could coerce or manipulate Him. What do the following Scriptures teach us about the sovereignty and power of God? Is there any created being or thing that can "change" God?

a. *Isaiah 14:24*

_____

_____

_____

_____

b. *Isaiah 46:9-10*

_____

_____

c. *Daniel 4:34-35*

Chapter 13: God Is Omnipotent

The word "omnipotent" comes from the Latin word **omnipotens** [**omnis** = all + **potens** = powerful] and refers to the attribute of having infinite or unlimited power. With regard to God, the word means that He can do all that He has determined to do, and no person or force can hinder Him or oblige Him to do the contrary. To say that God can do all things means that He can do all that is in agreement with His most holy, righteous, and loving nature. He **cannot** contradict Himself—He cannot be cruel or selfish; He cannot lie; He cannot break a promise; He cannot do the absurd (*e.g.* make square circles, triangles with four corners, or rocks so heavy that He cannot move them). For the Christian, the omnipotence of God instills absolute confidence. God is powerful to do all that He has promised. For the unbeliever, the omnipotence of God instills terror, because no man can resist His will or escape His judgment.

1. In the Scripture, a person's name has great significance in that it often reveals something about his or her character. What are the names and titles given to God in the following Scriptures?

    a. *God A_____ (Genesis 17:1; Revelation 4:8; 19:6).*

    b. *The Lord S_____ and M_____ (Psalm 24:8).*

    c. *A R_____ of Strength (Psalm 31:2).*

    d. *A T_____ of S_____ (Psalm 61:3).*

    e. *M_____ God (Isaiah 9:6; Isaiah 10:21).*

    f. *The M_____ One (Luke 1:49).*

2. What do the following Scriptures teach about the omnipotence of God? Is there anything beyond the power of God?

    a. *Jeremiah 32:17, 27*

    _____

    _____

    _____

    _____

    _____

b. *Matthew 19:26 (Luke 1:37)*

_____

_____

_____

_____

_____

_____

3. One of the most important implications of the omnipotence of God is that it assures us that He is able to carry out all that He has determined to do. What do the following Scriptures teach us about this truth?

a. *Job 42:1-2*

_____

_____

_____

_____

b. *Psalm 115:3*

_____

_____

_____

_____

c. *Psalm 135:5-6*

_____

_____

_____

_____

d. *Isaiah 14:24, 27*

_____

_____

_____

_____

e. *Daniel 4:35*

_____

_____

_____

_____

f. *Ephesians 1:11*

_____

_____

_____

_____

4. In the Scriptures, the omnipotence of God is one of the attributes that most distinguishes Him from the lifeless idols that men are so prone to create. Read Psalm 115:3-11, and then answer the following questions.

a. *In Psalm 115:3-8, how is the omnipotent God of the Scriptures contrasted with the worthless idols of men?*

_____

_____

_____
_____
_____
_____

b. *According to Psalm 115:9-11, how should believers respond to this truth?*

_____
_____
_____
_____
_____
_____

5. The omnipotence of God has great implications for the Christian who trusts in Him, His will, and His promises. According to the following Scriptures, what does the omnipotence of God mean for those of us who believe?

a. *Joshua 23:14*

_____
_____
_____
_____

b. *Psalm 121:4-5*

_____
_____

c. *Romans 8:31*

d. *Philippians 1:6*

e. *II Corinthians 3:4-5*

f. *Philippians 4:13*

_____

_____

_____

_____

_____

6. According to the following Scriptures, the Christian's response to the omnipotence of God should be one of both faith and obedience. Write your thoughts on these passages and their respective emphases.

a. *Faith (Romans 4:19-21)*

_____

_____

_____

_____

_____

b. *Obedience (Genesis 17:1)*

_____

_____

_____

_____

_____

Chapter 14: God Is Omnipresent

The word "omnipresent" comes from the Latin word **omnipraesens** [**omnis** = all + **praesens** = present] and refers to the state of being present everywhere at once. When the Bible speaks of God as omnipresent, it means that He is always present in every place in His fullness. Omnipresence does not mean that part of God is in China and another part of God is in England, but that **all** of God is everywhere at once. Although the universe itself cannot contain God, God is present in all His fullness in every place. For the Christian, the omnipresence of God instills great confidence and comfort—every believer from the greatest to the smallest benefits from God's undivided presence. For the unbeliever, the omnipresence of God instills terror, because there is no possibility of hiding or escaping from His presence.

1. In I Kings 8 is found an account of the dedication of the temple of God that Solomon built in Jerusalem. What did Solomon declare in I Kings 8:27? What does his declaration teach us about the omnipresence of God? According to this text, should we think that God is somehow confined to our modern-day "church buildings"?

   _____

   _____

   _____

   _____

   _____

2. In the following Scriptures are found several important texts regarding the omnipresence of God and its implications for all men. Write a summary of each passage in your own words.

   a. *Psalm 139:7-10*

   _____

   _____

   _____

   _____

   _____

b. *Jeremiah 23:23-24*

_____

_____

_____

_____

c. *Acts 17:24-28*

_____

_____

_____

_____

_____

NOTES: The phrase, "in Him we live and move and exist [literally, 'are']," is extremely important (v.28). Whether man acknowledges it or not, the reality of God is inescapable. There is no place that He is not. Furthermore, all things were made by Him and continue to be sustained by Him. He set the universe in motion and sustains it. The most colossal star and the smallest particle exist because of Him. The life of every creature, great or small, is dependent upon Him.

3. The following Scriptures contain fundamental truths about the omnipresence of God with a special emphasis regarding its significance for His people. Summarize the truth of each text in your own words.

a. *Deuteronomy 4:7*

_____

_____

_____

_____

b. *Psalm 46:1*

c. *Psalm 145:18-19*

d. *Isaiah 43:1-2*

e. *Matthew 28:20*

Chapter 15: God Is Omniscient

The word "omniscience" comes from the Latin word **omnisciens** [**omnis** = all + **sciens**, from **scire** = to know] and refers to the attribute of possessing all knowledge. The omniscience of God indicates that He possesses perfect knowledge of all things past, present, and future—immediately, effortlessly, simultaneously, and exhaustively. There is nothing hidden from God. There is never the slightest difference between God's knowledge and what really is. He knows all the facts, and He interprets them with perfect wisdom. For the Christian, the omniscience of God instills great confidence and comfort—God knows our every need, He understands our every trial, and He has given us His infallible Word to guide us through life. For the unbeliever, the omniscience of God instills terror, because God will judge every man according to His perfect knowledge of all the facts—no sin is hidden or will be forgotten. Every creature, every deed, and every thought is before Him like an open book.

1. In the Scriptures, a name has great significance and communicates something about the person who bears it. What is the name given to God in I Samuel 2:3?

   a. *The God of K_____.*

   b. *What does this name communicate to us about God's omniscience?*

   _____

   _____

   _____

   _____

   NOTES: The Lord is the God who sees and knows all things. Knowledge is not something that God must attain, search for, or gather; but it is something that He always possesses perfectly, immediately, effortlessly, simultaneously, and exhaustively.

2. In Daniel 2:20-22 is found one of Scripture's most beautiful descriptions of the knowledge of God. What does this text teach us?

   _____

   _____

   _____

_____

_____

_____

3. In the following Scriptures, several words are used to describe God's omniscience. Through our understanding of these words, we can begin to grasp something of the greatness of God's knowledge. Identify each word according to the verse given.

   a. *God's knowledge is P*_____ *(Job 37:16).* The word is translated from the Hebrew word **tamim**, which denotes that which is whole, complete, entire, blameless, and lacking in nothing.

   b. *God's understanding is I*_____ *(Psalm 147:4-5).* The word is translated from the Hebrew word **ayin**, which denotes that which is innumerable or beyond counting. Other synonyms include: endless, inscrutable, unfathomable, and unsearchable.

   c. *God's understanding is I*_____ *(Isaiah 40:28).* The word is translated from the Hebrew word **ayin** (see definition above).

4. It is important to understand that God's knowledge is not limited to the present; He knows all things past, present, and future. What do Isaiah 44:6-8 and 46:9-10 teach us about this truth?

_____

_____

_____

_____

_____

5. In Psalm 139:1-4, 11-12 is found one of the most beautiful and thorough descriptions of the omniscience of God and His knowledge of the deeds of men. According to the outline given below, describe the extent of God's omniscience.

   a. *Verse 1*

_____

_____

NOTES: God's knowledge reaches to the profoundest depth of a man's being. The deepest recesses of a man's heart and mind are like an open book before the Lord.

b. *Verse 2*

c. *Verse 3*

NOTES: The word "scrutinize" is translated from the Hebrew word **zarah**, which means, "to scatter, fan, or winnow." In the process of winnowing, the wheat is separated from the chaff. In a similar but infinitely more profound manner, God is able to winnow the hearts of man and discern every thought with perfect accuracy.

d. *Verse 4*

e. *Verses 11-12*

_____

_____

_____

_____

_____

6. According to the Scriptures, there is no depth or secret in the heart of man that is beyond the reach of God's knowledge. What do the following Scriptures teach us about this truth?

   a. *God alone knows the H_____ of all men (I Kings 8:39).*

   b. *God T_____ the H_____ and M_____ (Psalm 7:9).*

   c. *God knows the T_____ of man (Psalm 94:11).*

   d. *God will J_____ the S_____ of all men (Romans 2:16).*

7. For the Christian, the omniscience of God instills great confidence, comfort, and joy. We can rest secure that God is always watching us and that He knows our every need and understands our every trial. What do the following Scriptures teach us about this truth?

   a. *II Chronicles 16:9*

_____

_____

_____

_____

_____

   b. *Matthew 6:7-8, 31-32*

_____

_____

_____

_____

_____

c. _Matthew 10:29-31_

_____

_____

_____

_____

_____

8. As we have learned, the omniscience of God does not produce the same reaction in all men. Everything depends upon one's relationship with God. For the unbeliever, the omniscience of God instills terror, because God will judge every man according to His perfect knowledge of all the facts—no sin is hidden or will be forgotten. Every creature, every deed, and every thought is before Him like an open book. What do the following Scriptures teach us about this truth?

a. _Job 34:21-23_

_____

_____

_____

b. _Psalm 33:13-15_

_____

_____

_____

c. *Proverbs 5:21*

_____

_____

_____

_____

d. *Proverbs 15:3*

_____

_____

_____

_____

e. *Jeremiah 17:10; 32:19*

_____

_____

_____

_____

f. *Hebrews 4:13*

_____

_____

_____

_____

Chapter 16: God Is Holy

THE MEANING OF "HOLY"

The word "holy" comes from the Hebrew word **qadosh**, which means, "separated, marked off, placed apart, or withdrawn from common use." With regard to God, the word has two important meanings: God is transcendent above His creation and above His creation's corruption.

GOD IS TRANSCENDENT ABOVE HIS CREATION

The word "transcendence" comes from the Latin verb **transcendere** (**trans** = over + **scandere** = to climb), which means, "to go beyond, rise above, or exceed." As Creator, God is above His creation and totally distinct from every created being. The distinction between God and the rest of His creation is not merely quantitative (the same, but greater), but qualitative (God is a completely different Being). Regardless of their splendor, all other beings on earth and in heaven are mere creatures. God alone is God—separate, transcendent, and unapproachable.

Holiness is the preeminent attribute of God and the greatest truth that we can ever learn about Him. Every other divine attribute that we have studied and will study is simply an expression of His holiness in that it demonstrates that He is distinct from His creation and absolutely separate—a completely different Being. The triune nature of God is an expression of His holiness—is there any created being so incomprehensible, mysterious, and wonderful? To say that God is spirit is to express another aspect of His holiness—is there any created being so free and unhindered? God's perfection, eternal nature, self-existence, immutability, omnipotence, omnipresence, and omniscience are all expressions of His holiness—is there any created being so great and worthy of reverence? As we continue our study of the attributes of God and as we walk before Him, we must keep in mind this one great truth—God is holy, and all that He is and does is an expression of His holiness!

GOD IS TRANSCENDENT ABOVE CREATION'S CORRUPTION

The holiness of God means that He transcends the moral corruption of His creation and is separated from all that is profane and sinful. God cannot sin, cannot take pleasure in sin, and cannot have fellowship with sin. It is impossible to overemphasize the importance of God's holiness. What we understand about this attribute will influence every aspect of our relationship with God. As the Scriptures declare in Proverbs 9:10, "The knowledge of the Holy One is understanding."

THE HOLINESS OF GOD

It is important to understand that God's holiness is **intrinsic** or **inherent** (*i.e.* inward, essential, or belonging to His nature). Holiness is not merely something that God decides to be or do; it is essential to who He is—He **is** holy. God would have to cease to be God in order to be unholy. He would have to deny His own nature to do something that is unholy. This is a wonderful truth that inspires great confidence in God.

1. In the Scriptures, a name has great significance and communicates something about the person who bears it. What are the names given to God in the following Scriptures, and what do they communicate to us about His holiness?

   a. *I A_____ Who I A_____ (Exodus 3:14).* God is holy, separate, and distinct from all other beings and things. There is no adequate illustration or example to communicate who He truly is. If we ask another man to describe himself to us, he can point to other human beings and say, "I am like him" or "I am like her." In contrast, God is incomparable. Not even the greatest archangel in heaven is an adequate example of who He is. When Moses asked God, "Who are You?" God could only point to Himself and declare: "I AM WHO I AM." This truth helps us to understand the great importance of the revelation of God in Christ. Jesus is God in the flesh and the only true image or example of who God is (John 14:9; Colossians 1:15). God now answers every question about Himself by pointing to His Son and declaring, "I am like Him!"

   b. *H_____ and A_____ is His name (Psalm 111:9).* The word "awesome" comes from the Hebrew verb **yare**, which means, "to fear." In this context, it denotes that God inspires awe and reverence. A proper understanding of the holiness of God will always result in a profound reverence before God.

   c. *The H_____ and E_____ One Who lives forever, whose name is H_____ (Isaiah 57:15).*

   d. *In the preceding verses, words such as "holy," "awesome," and "exalted" were used to describe God. What do these words communicate to you about the holiness of God?*

   _____

   _____

   _____

   _____

   _____

   _____

   _____

   _____

2. In the Scriptures, we find that the holiness of God is both preeminent and transcendent. It is **preeminent** in that no other divine attribute is so often declared and explained in the Scriptures. It is **transcendent** in that there is simply no comparison between the holiness of God and that of any other being or thing.

a. **GOD'S HOLINESS IS PREEMINENT** [Latin: **prae** = before + **eminere** = to project]. It is impossible to understand the character of God apart from His holiness. Above all things, God is holy! How is this truth demonstrated in Isaiah 6:3 and Revelation 4:8?

_____

_____

_____

_____

_____

_____

_____

NOTES: In Hebrew literature, repetition is used to give emphasis to what is being said. That God's holiness is declared three times (called the **trihagion** [Greek: **trís** = thrice + **hágios** = holy]) denotes that God is absolutely and infinitely holy. No other divine attribute is proclaimed with greater emphasis. We never read in the Scriptures that God is "love, love, love" or "merciful, merciful, merciful"; but we do read that He is "holy, holy, holy." Holiness is the foundation of all that God is and does. If there is one attribute of God that we simply cannot overemphasize, it is His holiness.

b. **GOD'S HOLINESS IS TRANSCENDENT** [Latin: **trans** = across or beyond + **scandere** = to climb]. God's holiness infinitely surpasses all others. There is none holy like the Lord! What do the following Scriptures teach us with regard to this truth?

(1) Exodus 15:11

_____

_____

_____

_____

(2) I Samuel 2:2

_____

_____

_____

_____

_____

(3) Job 15:15

_____

_____

_____

_____

_____

NOTES: This does not mean that there is sin or corruption in heaven but communicates two great truths: (1) nothing, not even the heavens themselves or those who dwell there, is holy like God; and (2) God's holiness alone is **_intrinsic_** or **_inherent_** (_i.e._ inward, essential, belonging to His nature). Holiness is not merely something that God decides to be or do; it is essential to who He is—He _is_ holy. In contrast, all other beings and things (even heaven and its holy angels) derive their holiness from God. They are not holy in themselves, but their holiness flows from God as a gift of grace to them. If God turned away from them and withdrew His grace, they would fall from their holy state into sin and corruption.

(4) Isaiah 40:25

_____

_____

_____

_____

3. The holiness of God means not only that He is unique among all His creation, but also that He is separated from all that is sinful. God cannot sin, cannot take pleasure in sin, and cannot have fellowship with sin. There is no possibility that God could be tempted or that His nature could be defiled. He always remains as He is—**holy** and **incorruptible**. What do the following Scriptures teach us about this truth?

a. *Psalm 5:4*

_____

_____

_____

_____

NOTES: The word "dwells" is translated from the Hebrew word **gur**, which literally means, "to sojourn." God has nothing to do with evil or wickedness. He has no fellowship with that which is morally unclean.

b. *Job 34:10*

_____

_____

_____

_____

c. *Isaiah 59:1-2*

_____

_____

_____

_____

NOTES: Here the intolerance of God toward sin is revealed. Because God is holy and righteous, outstanding sin will always lead to separation between God and the sinner. It is for this reason that God sent His only Son to pay our sin debt that He might have unbroken fellowship with us through faith (Romans 5:1).

d. *Habakkuk 1:13a*

_____

_____

_____

_____

e. *James 1:13*

_____

_____

_____

_____

NOTES: To say that God cannot be tempted does not mean merely that God has the moral fortitude to resist all temptation to evil; rather, it means that when evil presents itself to God there is nothing to resist. Because He is inherently and absolutely holy, all evil is an abomination to Him and does not appeal to Him in any way. He is not drawn to evil, nor does He have any need to resist it, because He abhors it through and through.

f. *James 1:17*

_____

_____

_____

_____

NOTES: No matter how long one observes God's person, Word, or works—even under the strictest standard of holiness and righteousness—not even the minutest flaw will ever be found. He dwells in unapproachable light in which there is not even the slightest tint or shadow of evil.

g. *I John 1:5*

_____

_____

_____

_____

4. The holiness of God means not only that He is unique among all His creation and that He is separated from all that contradicts His nature (*i.e.* sin), but also that He cannot take pleasure in sin. God is not neutral or apathetic about evil; it is an abomination (*i.e.* a loathsome thing that evokes hatred or disgust) to Him. He hates all that is evil with a holy passion. What do the following Scriptures teach us about this truth?

a. *Deuteronomy 25:16*

_____

_____

_____

_____

NOTES: The word "abomination" in this passage is from the Hebrew word **toeba**, which refers to something or someone who is repugnant (*i.e.* offensive), disgusting, revolting, or obscene. In Psalm 88:8, the word is translated, "object of loathing."

b. *Psalm 5:4-5*

_____

_____

_____

_____

NOTES: The popular saying, "God loves the sinner but hates the sin," must be interpreted in light of Psalm 5:5. God not only hates the sin, but His hatred is also manifested against those who practice it! How can this truth be reconciled with other passages of Scripture that speak of God's love for sinners? Though God's wrath is revealed against the sinner (John 3:36), He has demonstrated His love by sending His Son to die for the very people who deserve only judgment (Romans 5:8, 10). There is a genuine love of God toward all men, and this love is manifested in innumerable ways. Nevertheless, God is holy and His wrath (*i.e.* holy and just displeasure) will eventually be manifested toward all who reject salvation through Christ's atoning sacrifice.

c. *Proverbs 15:8-9*

_____

_____

_____

_____

NOTES: The word "abomination" in this passage is from the Hebrew word **toeba**, as in Deuteronomy 25:16 above.

Chapter 17: Our Response to the Holiness of God

God is holy, holy, holy! Although we have sinned against Him and made ourselves an abomination before Him, He has reconciled us who believe to Himself through the death of His own Son. Having saved us, He has called us to be His special people upon the earth. How shall we live in response to this great truth? How shall we live before a holy God?

THE IMPORTANCE OF HOLINESS

It would be difficult to overemphasize the need for us to understand the importance of the holiness of God and its implications for our lives. God is holy, and we are called to be holy as He is holy (I Peter 1:15-16).

1. According to Proverbs 9:10, how important is it that we acknowledge and understand the holiness of God? How important is it that we grow in our own personal holiness?

_____

_____

_____

NOTES: In Proverbs 9:10, we learn that the greatest truth set before men is that God is holy and worthy of all reverence and worship. All other knowledge and wisdom (scientific, philosophical, historical, legal, etc.) is worthless apart from a correct understanding of this truth.

2. According to Hebrews 12:14, how important is it that we grow in our own personal holiness?

_____

_____

_____

NOTES: The word "sanctification" comes from the Greek word *hagiasmós*, which can also be translated, "holiness" or "consecration." According to the Scriptures, the absolute holiness needed to see the Lord or be in His presence cannot be achieved through human merit but only through faith in Jesus Christ and His death on the cross. For this reason, the author of Hebrews also writes, "For by one offering He [*i.e.* Jesus] has perfected for all time those who are sanctified." However, in Hebrews 12:14, the truth being communicated is that all those who truly have been "perfected" or "sanctified" by the blood of Christ will also seek to be holy in their personal lives. We are not right with God **because** of our pursuit of holiness; rather, salvation by grace through faith will **lead** to our pursuit of holiness.

3. According to Hebrews 12:5-11, what does God do to ensure that **all** His children share in His holiness (*i.e.* become holy as He is holy)?

_____

_____

_____

_____

_____

NOTES: There are several important truths that we must recognize about God's discipline of His children. (1) God's discipline is an expression of His love and is always for the believer's good. (2) God's discipline is not retributive; its purpose is to protect us, mature us, and mold us into the image of Christ. (3) God's discipline can occur in a believer's life as a result of sin. In such cases, the purpose is to correct him, to prove to him the dangers of sin, and to teach him reverence for God. (4) God's discipline can occur in the life of even the most mature and pious believer. In such cases, it is simply to take him to greater heights of conformity to Christ. (5) God's discipline can be terribly painful, but afterwards it yields the fruit of greater righteousness and holiness. (6) God's discipline in our lives is evidence that we are His children. Lack of discipline is evidence that we are not. (7) God's great goal for our present lives is not material prosperity, comfort, or even health, but that we may share in His holiness (12:10).

OUR RESPONSE TO THE HOLINESS OF GOD

God is holy, holy, holy! In light of this great truth, we must ask ourselves: "How then shall we live?" In the following, we will consider several of the most important biblical responses to the holiness of God. We must always keep in mind that the study of the attributes of God is not merely an intellectual pursuit, but it should have the greatest impact upon our **doxology** (*i.e.* worship) and our **praxis** (*i.e.* actions or behavior).

REVERENCE AND GODLY FEAR

1. In Psalm 96:9 is found one of the most beautiful commands in all of Scripture regarding the believer's responsibility before the Lord. Summarize its meaning in your own words.

_____

_____

_____

_____

NOTES: The word "attire" comes from the Hebrew word **hadarah**, which may also be translated, "beauty" or "splendor." The same phrase is found in Psalm 96:9; 110:3; I Chronicles 16:29; and II Chronicles 20:21. There is a debate as to whether the psalmist is referring to the holiness of God or the holiness of the one who is worshiping. If it is the former, then it is a call for us to worship God because of the beauty of His holiness. If it is the latter, it is a call for us to come before God with a pure heart and a holy life. This is true beauty in the eyes of God. The call to tremble is not because God is capricious or untrustworthy, but because of the infinite greatness of His holiness and power.

2. In Isaiah 6:2-3, we are granted a glimpse into the very throne room of God. What can we learn from this scene of heavenly worship?

_____

_____

_____

_____

NOTES: The Scriptures do not reveal a great deal about the angelic creatures called "seraphim." However, because of their proximity to God's throne, it is logical to suppose that they are possibly the greatest of all creatures in holiness and power. Nevertheless, in the presence of God they can only bow their heads and worship. There have been many opinions put forth regarding the symbolism of their wings. It is possible that they cover their faces in reverence or because the glory of God is too much even for them to bear. They cover their feet in humility recognizing that they are mere creatures and the Lord alone is God.

3. In Isaiah 8:13, three duties are given regarding the believer's relationship to the Lord. Read the text, and identify these duties by filling in the blanks.

   a. *We should regard Him as H_____.* The phrase "regard as holy" comes from the single Hebrew word **qadash**, which literally means, "to set apart or consecrate." We are to set God apart in our hearts as separate or distinct from all other persons and things. He is to have first place in our lives with no other competing desires or loyalties.

   b. *He shall be our F_____.* The word "fear" comes from the Hebrew word **morah**, which denotes fear, terror, reverence, or awe. Fear and terror are often associated with unrighteousness or wickedness. Evil and evil men instill terror in us. However, when the word is used of God, it is a fear that results from His infinite majesty, beauty, holiness, righteousness, and power.

   c. *He shall be our D_____.* The word "dread" comes from the Hebrew word **arats**, which means, "to cause terror, shock, dread, or awe." From the context (v.12), we learn that God is admonishing His people not to fear men and thus compromise their faith; rather, they are to fear Him and follow Him with all their hearts. Then He will be a sanctuary for His people and protect them from their enemies (v.14).

4. Habakkuk 2:20 and Ecclesiastes 5:1-2 are two important texts that communicate to us something of the reverence required when approaching God to pray or worship. Summarize the meaning of both texts, and explain how the truths they convey can be applied to our own lives.

_____

_____

_____

_____

_____

_____

NOTES: These texts do not intend to discourage prayer or worship. Nor does God intend that we be so afraid of speaking something incorrect that it paralyzes us so that we cannot pray or worship. Both texts simply communicate the need for a biblical reverence or fear when approaching God. We should draw confidence from the fact that God is our Father, and yet we must keep in mind that our Father is God. When we pray or worship, we are coming before "the King eternal, immortal, invisible, the only God, to whom belongs honor and glory forever and ever" (I Timothy 1:17).

WORSHIP, GLADNESS, AND THANKSGIVING

1. What do the following texts admonish us to do in response to the holiness of God? How should we obey these admonitions in our daily life?

   a. *Psalm 30:4*

   b. *Psalm 97:12*

   c. *Psalm 99:3, 5, 9*

NOTES: God's holy hill (v.9) is a reference to the city of Jerusalem (43:3; 48:1; 87:1). In the Old Covenant, this was the location appointed for God's temple. This no longer applies to the believer. As Jesus told the Samaritan woman: "An hour is coming when neither in this mountain nor in Jerusalem will you worship the Father... But an hour is coming, and now is, when the true worshipers will worship the Father in spirit and truth; for such people the Father seeks to be His worshipers" (John 4:21-23). God's footstool (v.5) may also be a reference to Jerusalem (I Chronicles 28:2) or to the whole earth. In Isaiah 66:1, God declares: "Heaven is My throne, and the earth is My footstool. Where then is a house you could build for Me?"

d. *Isaiah 12:6*

_____

_____

_____

_____

2. In Revelation 15:3-4 is recorded the song of Moses and the song of the Lamb. What are the reasons given as to why all men should worship God? How can this be applied to our own lives as believers?

_____

_____

_____

_____

_____

HOLINESS AND OBEDIENCE

1. In Leviticus 20:26 is found one of the most foundational truths about the believer's relationship with God. What has God done for us, and how are we to respond?

_____

_____

_____

_____

_____

NOTES: God has set us apart from the rest of the peoples on the earth to be His. We are to respond by separating ourselves from all that displeases Him and by giving ourselves to Him in worship and service.

2. In Leviticus 22:31-33, the same truths that we discovered in Leviticus 20:26 are revealed to us with even greater depth. What has God done for us, and how are we to respond?

_____

_____

_____

_____

_____

NOTES: The word "sanctified" comes from the Hebrew word **qudash**, which means, "to set apart or consecrate." God has sanctified us to be His special people. We are to sanctify the Lord (*i.e.* set Him apart above all) by keeping His commandments. The word "pollute" comes from the Hebrew word **chalal**, which means, "to defile or pollute." To break God's commands is to profane His name. The foundation of God's claim upon Israel and the reason why Israel should have honored Him was the fact that He had redeemed them from the bondage of slavery in the land of Egypt. How much more should we honor God, who has redeemed us from the bondage of sin by the blood of His own Son?

3. It is important to understand that the admonition to holiness is not just an Old Testament idea or standard, but it is also found throughout the New Testament. Write your thoughts on the following texts. How should we respond to God's holiness?

   a. *II Corinthians 6:16-18*

_____

_____

_____

_____

_____

b. *II Corinthians 7:1*

_____

_____

_____

_____

NOTES: The word "flesh" comes from the Greek word **sárx**, which in this context probably refers to our physical bodies. The phrase "flesh and spirit" refers to the totality of who we are. We are to strive to cleanse ourselves of every kind of sin in every area of our lives—thoughts, attitudes, words, and deeds. The word "perfecting" is translated from the Greek verb **epiteléō**, which means, "to complete or accomplish." The phrase "perfecting holiness" refers to our growth in personal holiness. Negatively, we cleanse ourselves from the sin that defiles us. Positively, we strive toward greater heights of holiness or conformity to God. The motivation for this is not only the love of God manifested in our redemption but also our fear or reverence toward God.

c. *I Peter 1:14-17*

_____

_____

_____

_____

Chapter 18: God Is Righteous

THE MEANING OF "RIGHTEOUS"

The word "righteous" is translated from the Hebrew word **tsaddiq** and the corresponding Greek word **díkaios**. Both terms denote the rightness, correctness, or moral excellence of God. According to the Scriptures, God is an absolutely righteous Being and always acts in a way that is perfectly consistent with who He is. There is nothing wrong or incorrect about God's nature or His works. He will never "be" or "do" anything that would justify any accusation of wrongdoing. His works, decrees, and judgments are absolutely perfect. On the day when God judges all men according to their works, even the condemned will bow their heads and declare that God is right!

THE RIGHTEOUSNESS OF GOD

It is important to understand that God's righteousness is **intrinsic** or **inherent** (*i.e.* inward, essential, belonging to His nature). Righteousness is not merely something that God decides to be or do; it is essential to His very nature—He **is** righteous. God would have to cease to be God in order to be unrighteous. He would have to deny His own nature to do something that is not right. This is a wonderful truth that inspires great confidence in God.

1. In the Scriptures, a name has great significance and communicates something about the person who bears it. What is the name given to God in Psalm 7:9?

   a. *The R_____ God (Psalm 7:9).*

   b. *What does this name communicate to us about God's person and works?*

   _____

   _____

   _____

   _____

   NOTES: At the risk of being redundant, the important truth communicated here is that God **is** righteous; therefore, all His decrees, words, and deeds are perfectly righteous and worthy of absolute trust.

2. In the following verses are some of the most important declarations in the Scriptures with regard to the righteousness of God and His works. Summarize each text in your own words.

Remember: there is a direct relationship between God's righteous nature and the righteousness of His acts and judgments. God **does** right and **judges** righteously because God **is** righteous.

a. *Deuteronomy 32:4*

_____

_____

_____

_____

b. *Job 36:22-24*

_____

_____

_____

_____

c. *Psalm 36:6*

_____

_____

_____

_____

NOTES: The metaphors are clear. God's righteousness is greater than the highest mountain and more profound than the deepest sea.

d. *Psalm 89:14; 97:2*

_____

_____

_____

_____

e. *Psalm 119:142*

_____

_____

_____

_____

NOTES: Here we see two great truths. First, God's righteousness is immutable—it is everlasting and unchanging. He will always be righteous and absolutely trustworthy. Secondly, the truthfulness of God's Word is founded upon the righteousness of His character. We know the Word *is* truth because we know its Author *is* righteous.

f. *Jeremiah 9:24*

_____

_____

_____

_____

3. It is important to understand that the justice of God (like His holiness) is **transcendent** [Latin: **trans** = across or beyond + **scandere** = to climb]. God's righteousness infinitely surpasses all others. There is no other who is righteous like the Lord. What do the following Scriptures teach us about this truth?

a. *Isaiah 5:16*

_____

_____

_____

NOTES: This Scripture demonstrates that the Holy God will show Himself to be separate or distinct from all others through His righteousness. God's holiness (*i.e.* separateness, distinctiveness from creation) is most clearly demonstrated through His righteous deeds. There is none holy or righteous like the Lord.

b. *Isaiah 45:21*

_____

_____

_____

_____

4. It is important to understand that the righteousness of God, like His holiness, is reflected in His attitude toward the deeds of men and angels. God is not morally neutral or apathetic; He loves righteousness and hates all unrighteousness. What do the following Scriptures teach us about this truth?

a. *Psalm 7:11-12*

_____

_____

_____

_____

b. *Psalm 11:7*

_____

_____

_____

_____

NOTES: Both of the above texts demonstrate every man's great need of Christ and His work on Calvary. God is perfectly righteous and will judge all that fall short of His standard. Christ alone lived the perfect life that we could not live and then bore our sin and suffered the wrath of God that is described in Psalm 7:11-12. Psalm 11:7 declares that only the upright will behold God's face. Such righteousness is only possible through faith in the person and work of Christ. In II Corinthians 5:21, the Apostle Paul writes: "He made Him who knew no sin to be sin on our behalf, so that we might become the righteousness of God in Him."

5. The righteousness of God guarantees that God will do no wrong. He will rule over His creation without caprice, partiality, or injustice. This is a great comfort for the believer who has made God his hope. What do the following Scriptures teach us about this truth?

   a. *II Chronicles 19:7*

   _____

   _____

   _____

   _____

   b. *Job 8:3; 36:23*

   _____

   _____

   _____

   _____

   c. *Psalm 9:7-8*

   _____

   _____

   _____

   _____

Chapter 19: Our Response to the Righteousness of God

God is righteous, and all His works are perfect. How then shall we live in response to this great truth? We should fear the Lord and live righteously before Him; we should live with the greatest confidence in His providence; we should devote ourselves to worship and prayer; and finally, we should proclaim His righteousness among the people.

WE SHOULD LIVE RIGHTEOUSLY BEFORE GOD

1. In I John 2:29 and 3:7 is found a fundamental truth of the Christian life. According to these two texts, what is one of the greatest evidences that we are truly children of God?

_____

_____

_____

_____

_____

NOTES: To "practice righteousness" is to live according to the standard of God's righteousness—to live in a manner that conforms to His nature and will. It is important to understand that we do not gain a right standing before God by practicing righteousness; rather, our practice of righteousness is evidence that we have truly been born again. A genuine Christian is not sinless, but he will not live out all the days of his life in sin and rebellion. If someone professes to be a Christian, yet his or her life is marked by unrelenting disobedience to God's Word—without repentance or divine discipline—it is certain that his or her profession is not genuine.

2. In Ephesians 4:22-24, the Scriptures set out for us the way by which we might live a righteous life before God. Read the text until you are familiar with its contents, and then complete the following exercise.

   a. *We are to L_____ A_____ the old self (v.22).* In this context, the "old self" (literally, "old man") refers to the person that we were and the accompanying sinful lifestyle that we lived prior to conversion. Since we really have become new creatures in Christ (II Corinthians 5:17), we should and can put off the sinful deeds of the person that we used to be.

b. *We are to be R_____ in the spirit of our M_____* (v.23). This renewal of our minds is accomplished by the power of the Holy Spirit working through the Word. In Romans 12:2, we find a similar admonition: "And do not be conformed to this world, but be transformed by the renewing of your mind." The more we renew our minds in the Scriptures and the more we cultivate the mind of Christ, the more likely we are to lay aside the old self with its sinful habits and put on the new self that reflects the righteousness and holiness of God.

c. *We are to P_____ on the new self* (v.24). Having put off the old self with its sinful deeds, we must now put on, cultivate, or adorn ourselves in those deeds that are appropriate to our new life as children of God.

d. *According to verse 24, whose likeness does this new self reflect? Describe this likeness.*

_____

_____

_____

_____

NOTES: God's character is the pattern according to which we must now live—a life marked by righteousness and holiness, which is founded upon and flows from our knowledge of and submission to the truth.

WE SHOULD LIVE WITH GREAT CONFIDENCE IN GOD

1. The absolute righteousness of God is one of the greatest incentives to rely upon Him, even in the midst of trials. Because He is righteous, we can trust our lives to His every word and work. What do the following Scriptures teach us about this truth?

   a. *Psalm 92:15*

   _____

   _____

   _____

   _____

NOTES: In the Scriptures, the word "rock" is often used with reference to God (Deuteronomy 32:4; Psalm 18:2; 94:22). In such cases, it denotes trustworthiness, steadfastness, and strength. God is all these things to His people because He is "a God of faithfulness and without injustice; righteous and upright is He" (Deuteronomy 32:4).

b. *Isaiah 41:10*

_____

_____

_____

_____

2. The righteousness of God that leads us to trust in Him is also the foundation and incentive for prayer. What do the following texts from the Old and New Testaments teach us about this truth?

a. *Psalm 145:17-19*

_____

_____

_____

_____

b. *Luke 18:7-8*

_____

_____

_____

_____

NOTES: The question, "When the Son of Man comes, will He find faith on the earth?" is important. It proves that persevering faith and prayer are necessary for the appropriation of His promises.

WE SHOULD LIVE A LIFE OF WORSHIP TO GOD

1. In Psalm 96:11-13, we find one of the most powerful biblical admonitions to worship the Lord. According to this text, what should be our response to the righteousness of God?

_____

_____

_____

_____

2. In Revelation 15:3-4 is found an admonition very similar to that of Psalm 96:11-13. According to this text, what should be our response to the righteousness of God?

_____

_____

_____

_____

WE SHOULD PROCLAIM
GOD'S RIGHTEOUSNESS TO OTHERS

1. According to the Scriptures, not only are we to live righteously before God, trust in His righteousness, and worship Him for His righteous deeds; but also we are to proclaim His righteousness to all peoples both near and far. What do the following texts teach us with regard to this truth? How should we apply these truths to our lives?

    a. *Psalm 40:10*

_____

_____

_____

_____

b. *Psalm 71:15-16*

_____

_____

_____

_____

_____

_____

NOTES: Two great truths are presented before us. First, although we do not fully comprehend the sum of God's righteous deeds, this should not hinder us from telling others about what we do know. Second, we should speak much about God's righteous deeds and not our own. As the psalmist says, "Not to us, O LORD, not to us, but to Your name give glory" (Psalm 115:1).

c. *Psalm 145:6-7*

_____

_____

_____

_____

d. *Jeremiah 9:23-24*

_____

_____

_____

_____

NOTES: As we learned in Psalm 71:15-16, we are not to boast about our own righteousness or the things that we have done, but we are to boast in God's righteousness and His righteous deeds on the earth.

2. According to I Peter 2:9-10, what is one of the great purposes of the New Testament Church and the individual believer? How should we live in light of this truth?

_____

_____

_____

_____

_____

_____

NOTES: We are set on this earth to proclaim the moral excellencies of God to all men. We do this by our testimony, by teaching His Word, and by living a life that demonstrates His power. This is not only an obligation, but it is also a great privilege.

Chapter 20: God Is True

THE INTEGRITY OF GOD

The word "integrity" comes from the Latin word **integer**, which refers to anything complete or whole. When used with reference to God, the word means that God's character is whole, flawless, or unimpaired. There are three words that may be employed to describe God's integrity: (1) God is **true**—He is real, not fabricated, invented, or an imitation; (2) God is **truthful**—He only acts and speaks within the realm of the truth, and falsehood is contrary to His nature; and (3) God is **faithful**—He always fulfills all of His promises.

GOD IS TRUE OR GENUINE

In the Scriptures, the word "true" is translated from the Hebrew word **'emet** and the Greek word **alēthinós**. Both words denote not only the truthfulness of God but also His authenticity. God is genuine or real. He is exactly as He reveals Himself to be. He is not a counterfeit, a fake, an invention, or a mere imitation. He is the one true and living God—distinct from the idols made by the hands of men and the false gods born in the corrupt imaginations of men.

1. In the Scriptures, a name is often the means through which the character of a person is revealed. What are the names ascribed to God in the following Scriptures? What do they reveal about His authenticity? Write your thoughts.

   a. *But the LORD is the T_____ God; He is the L_____ God and the everlasting King (Jeremiah 10:10).*

   _____

   _____

   _____

   _____

   _____

   NOTES: The word "true" comes from the Hebrew word **'emet**. It denotes not only that God is true but also that He is faithful. The adjective "living" is translated from the Hebrew word **chay** and is often used to contrast the true God with lifeless idols.

b. The O_____ T_____ God (John 17:3).

_____

_____

_____

_____

_____

NOTES: Jesus uses two powerful adjectives to prove the authenticity of God. He is truly God, and He is the one and only true God. It is important to note that Jesus is not denying His own deity; rather, He is speaking as the Mediator between God and man. The fact that Jesus puts Himself in a conjunctive relationship with the Father and declares that the purpose of eternal life is to also know Him is proof of His deity. If He were not deity, such language would be wholly inappropriate—even blasphemous.

c. The L_____ and T_____ God (I Thessalonians 1:9).

_____

_____

_____

_____

d. The Lord H_____ and T_____ (Revelation 6:10).

_____

_____

_____

_____

2. What do the following Scriptures teach us about the uniqueness and authenticity of God? Is there any true and living God other than the God of the Scriptures?

   a. *II Samuel 7:22*

   _____

   _____

   _____

   _____

   b. *I Kings 8:60*

   _____

   _____

   _____

   _____

   NOTES: This declaration occurs in Solomon's benediction after his prayer for the newly constructed temple. It demonstrates Solomon's true motive for asking God to bless His people—that all the peoples of the earth might know that the Lord is God and there is no one else.

   c. *Isaiah 46:9*

   _____

   _____

   _____

   _____

3. To fully understand the significance and importance of the truth we have learned, we must consider the Scriptures that contrast the living God with the lifeless idols and false gods of men. What do the following Scriptures teach us about the uniqueness and authenticity of God compared to false gods and lifeless idols?

a. *Psalm 115:3-9*

_____

_____

_____

_____

_____

b. *Isaiah 46:5-10*

_____

_____

_____

_____

_____

4. In Jeremiah 10:3-16 is found an excellent comparison between the one true and living God and the lifeless idols and false gods of men. Read the text until you are familiar with its contents, and then continue with the following exercise.

a. *How are the lifeless idols and false gods of men described in this passage?*

(1) Idols are nothing more than a D_____ (vv.3, 8). This comes from the Hebrew word **hebel**, which literally means, "vapor" or "breath." Thus, it signifies a vanity or a delusion. Idols are such because they are supposed to be powerful divine beings, when in fact they are not even alive.

(2) Idols are nothing more than W_____ cut from the forest (vv.3, 8). The man who worships an idol worships a lifeless tree. The crown of God's creation is reduced to worshiping a lifeless and mindless plant.

(3) Idols are nothing more than the W_____ of man—a craftsman with a cutting tool (vv.3, 9). Men refuse to worship the God who made them and instead worship the gods they make themselves (Romans 1:21-23).

(4) Idols are mere decorations of S_____ and G_____ (vv.4, 9). An idol is nothing more than a piece of wood, entirely without intrinsic splendor. For this reason,

it must be decorated and adorned externally. God's beauty and majesty are not a veneer; they are intrinsic or inherent. They emanate from who He really is.

(5) Idols are fastened nails so that they will not T_____ (v.4). The word "totter" comes from the Hebrew word **puq**, which means, "to reel, wobble, or totter so as to fall." Idols totter and fall over at the slightest nudge, but the one true God upholds the entire universe with the word of His power (Hebrews 1:3).

(6) Idols are like a S_____ in a cucumber field (v.5). A scarecrow was usually made of straw, thatch, or palm leaves. It was dry, brittle, and lifeless—a pathetic replica or hollow caricature of a man, able to deceive only the most gullible of the lower beasts. If a scarecrow fails miserably to represent a man, how can an idol represent God?

(7) Idols cannot S_____, and they must be C_____ because they cannot walk (v.5). Idols are mute and lame. Even wicked men can boast about power that they do not possess, but idols cannot even vainly boast. The fact that idols must be carried demonstrates their impotence and uselessness. The true God carries His people. In Deuteronomy 1:31, Moses declared, "The LORD your God carried you, just as a man carries his son" (see also Deuteronomy 32:11).

(8) Idols can do neither H_____ nor G_____ to us (v.5). For this reason, idols are neither to be feared for the punishment that their devotees pretend that they can inflict, nor to be adored and thanked for the good that is wrongly attributed to them.

(9) Idols are D_____ and there is no B_____ in them (v.14). The word "deceitful" is translated from the Hebrew word **sheqer**, which also means, "deception, disappointment, falsehood, or lie." An idol that has no breath cannot give life to men. But the true and living God gives life and breath to all (Job 33:4; 34:14-15). For this reason, everything that has breath should praise the Lord (Psalm 150:6).

(10) Idols are W_____ (v.15). This word is translated from the Hebrew word **hebel**, which literally means, "vapor" or "breath." Thus, it denotes something that is a vain or worthless delusion.

(11) Idols are a W_____ of M_____ that will perish under the judgment of God (v.15). The word "mockery" is translated from the Hebrew word **tatuim**. There are two possible meanings: (1) idols are mere objects to be mocked (NET), or (2) they are a delusion to those who trust in them (ESV). Both ideas are true.

b. *How are idolaters (namely, those who trust in and reverence idols) described in this passage?*

(1) Verse 8

_____

_____

_____

_____

NOTES: The word "stupid" comes from the Hebrew word **baar**, which may also be translated, "brutish" or "senseless." The word "foolish" comes from the Hebrew word **kasal**, which may also be translated, "stupid." Both words are harsh but true descriptions of men who worship, serve, and care for lifeless idols that have been made with their own hands.

(2) Verse 14

_____

_____

_____

_____

NOTES: The word "stupid" comes from the Hebrew word **baar** (see definition above). Those who worship idols are without knowledge, void of knowledge, or aloof from knowledge. They are ignorant of truth and have little grasp upon reality.

c. _How is the true and living God of the Scriptures described in the following verses? How is He contrasted with the idols and false gods of men?_

(1) Verses 6-7

_____

_____

_____

_____

(2) Verse 10

_____

_____

(3) Verses 12-13

5. In light of what we have learned about the glory of the one true God and the vanity of dumb idols and false gods, how should we live? What do the following Scriptures teach us?

a. *Exodus 20:3; 23:13*

b. *Exodus 20:4-5, 23; Leviticus 19:4*

c. *I Thessalonians 1:9*

_____

_____

d. *I John 5:20-21*

_____

_____

_____

_____

6. It is extremely important to understand that idolatry can take many forms. If we give prefer-
ence to anyone or anything above God, then we are guilty of idolatry. The joys and pleasures
of this present world, careers, ministries, hobbies, and especially self are some of the more
common idols found among men. Prayerfully consider this truth and then answer the following questions. What is most dear to you? What most occupies your thought life? Do you think
most about the excellencies and glory of God, honoring God in your family, doing the will of
God in your vocation? Or do you think most about self, success, possessions, entertainment,
hobbies, and other things of this world? Are we not all guilty in some form or measure of idolatry? Do we not all have the need to repent and seek God's mercy and grace?

_____

_____

_____

_____

_____

_____

_____

_____

Chapter 21: God Is Truthful

Having considered the authenticity of God, we will now turn our attention toward His truthfulness. God is exactly as He reveals Himself to be (*i.e.* He is true); additionally, everything is always exactly as He says (*i.e.* He is truthful). God only acts and speaks within the realm of truth. His knowledge is perfect; He is therefore never mistaken. His character is holy and righteous; He therefore cannot lie or distort the truth. Misinterpretation and falsehood are impossible with God. This truth should promote in us the greatest confidence in God and His Word!

1. In the Scriptures, a name is the means through which the character of a person is revealed. What are the names and attributes ascribed to God in the following Scriptures?

   a. *The God of T_____ (Isaiah 65:16; Psalm 31:5).* In Isaiah 65:16, the word "truth" is translated from the Hebrew word **amen**. Literally, He is the God of the Amen—the God who says "amen" (*i.e.* "so be it") to all His promises. In Psalm 31:5, the word "truth" is translated from the Hebrew word **emeth**, which can also denote faithfulness.

   b. *God is T_____ (John 3:33).* This comes from the Greek word **alēthēs**, which may denote that God is real or genuine or that God is truthful. The context favors the latter.

   c. *Summarize in your own words what these names reveal to us about God's truthfulness. What impact should these things have on our lives?*

   _____

   _____

   _____

   _____

2. What do Numbers 23:19 and I Samuel 15:29 teach us about the truthfulness of God?

   _____

   _____

   _____

   _____

   _____

NOTES: God never lies, repents, or changes His purpose. He is not like men who continually change their minds, are often mistaken, and frequently distort the truth. God is true, and His Word is immutable (*i.e.* unchanging and unchangeable) truth.

3. The truthfulness of God has many great implications, but one of the most important is that we can trust in Him and His every promise. What do the following statements teach us about this truth?

   a. *God C_____ lie (Titus 1:2).* God cannot lie because He cannot do anything that would contradict His holy and righteous nature.

   b. *It is I_____ for God to L_____ (Hebrews 6:18).* The word "impossible" comes from the Greek word **adúnatos** [a = negative, no + **dunatós** = strong, mighty, powerful], which may also be translated, "unable" or "powerless."

   c. *What impact should the above Scriptures have on our lives? How should we live in light of them?*

   _____

   _____

   _____

   _____

   _____

   _____

4. Our God is the God of truth. Therefore, it is no surprise that His works and words are true. What do the following Scriptures teach us about this principle?

   a. *God's W_____ are T_____ (Daniel 4:37).* The word "true" comes from the Hebrew word **qeshot**, which is literally translated, "truth." The humbled king Nebuchadnezzar recognized that God's works were truth—even His judgments.

   b. *The W_____ of God's H_____ are T_____ (Psalm 111:7).* The word "truth" is translated from the Hebrew word **emeth**, which also denotes firmness or faithfulness.

   c. *The L_____ of God is T_____ (Psalm 119:142).* The word "truth" is translated from the Hebrew word **emeth** (see definition above).

   d. *All the C_____ of God are T_____ (Psalm 119:151).* The word "truth" is translated from the Hebrew word **emeth** (see definition above).

   e. *The S_____ of God's W_____ is T_____ (Psalm 119:160).* The word "truth" is translated from the Hebrew word **emeth** (see definition above).

f. *The Word of God is T_____ (John 17:17).* This comes from the Greek word **alêtheia**, which may also denote truthfulness and faithfulness.

5. Our God is the God of truth, and He has revealed His truth to men in various ways. According to the following Scriptures, what are the three principal ways through which God reveals truth to all men and especially to His people?

a. **GOD REVEALS HIS TRUTH THROUGH THE WORD OF GOD.** What does II Timothy 3:16-17 teach us about this truth?

_____

_____

_____

_____

NOTES: The word "inspired" comes from the Greek word **theópneustos**, which literally means, "God-breathed." Since the Scriptures "proceed out the mouth of God" (Matthew 4:4), they are totally reliable. It is important to note that the Scriptures not only teach the truth; but they also reprove us when we have strayed from the truth, give us correction so that we might return to the truth, and provide the training we need to be righteous.

b. **GOD REVEALS HIS TRUTH THROUGH HIS SON.** What do the following Scriptures teach us about this truth?

(1) John 1:14, 17

_____

_____

_____

_____

NOTES: The word "realized" in 1:17 comes from the Greek word **gínomai** and would probably be better translated, "came"—"grace and truth came through Jesus." John is not telling us that the Old Testament Law was bad or without grace and truth. He is simply stating that Jesus was a far superior revelation of grace and truth than the Law given through Moses could ever be.

(2) John 14:6

_____

_____

_____

_____

NOTES: This declaration is of great importance. Jesus is the greatest revelation of God's truth to man because **He is the truth**. He is not just a Teacher of the truth; He is the very embodiment of the truth. He is the very essence of all truth and the fountain of all truth. He is truth incarnate. To hear Him is to hear truth. To see Him is to see truth in action. In Ephesians 4:21, the Apostle Paul testifies that the truth is "in Jesus."

c. ***GOD REVEALS HIS TRUTH THROUGH THE HOLY SPIRIT.*** What do the following Scriptures teach us about this truth?

(1) The Holy Spirit is the S_____ of T_____ (John 14:16-17; 15:26; 16:13). Like the Father and the Son, truth is an attribute of the Holy Spirit and a characteristic of all that comes forth from Him. For this reason, the Apostle John draws a contrast in I John 4:6 between the spirit of truth and the spirit of error.

(2) The Holy Spirit guides God's people into all the T_____ (John 16:13). It is extremely important that we understand the immediate context of this verse. Jesus is speaking directly to His apostles, whom the Spirit would move to write the Holy Scriptures (II Peter 1:21). The Spirit's work through the apostles ensured that the New Testament Scriptures would be "inspired" or "God-breathed" and totally reliable (II Timothy 3:16). At the same time, the Spirit also leads God's people in the truth by illuminating their minds to understand the Scriptures (I Corinthians 2:12-13). It is important to remember that the Spirit will never guide the believer to any so-called truth that contradicts the grammar of what He has written in the Scriptures.

Chapter 22: Our Response to the Truthfulness of God

Our God is the God of truth; and all of His ways, works, and words are within the realm of truth. In the following Scriptures, we will consider how we as Christians should live in light of this truth.

WE SHOULD STUDY THE WORD OF TRUTH

1. In II Timothy 2:15, the Apostle Paul gave an important admonition to his young disciple Timothy regarding his relationship with the Scriptures. Describe this admonition, and explain how it should impact our own lives.

_____

_____

_____

_____

_____

_____

2. According to Psalm 1:1-3, what is the proper response of the believer to God's Word? What does God promise to those who give the proper place to His Word in their lives?

_____

_____

_____

_____

_____

_____

3. In the life of the scribe Ezra, we find a powerful example of a biblical response to God's truth. According to Ezra 7:10, what are the three things that Ezra set his heart to do? How should we follow Ezra's example?

WE SHOULD PRAY TO UNDERSTAND GOD'S TRUTH

1. In Psalm 25:4-5, what does David pray? How should we follow David's example?

---

2. Psalm 43 is a prayer of deliverance, yet in the midst of this prayer is a wonderful petition regarding God's truth. According to Psalm 43:3, what is this petition, and how should we apply it to our prayer life and study of God's Word?

---

3. We should pray not only to understand God's truth but also to obey it. What does Psalm 86:11 teach us with regard to this truth? How should we apply this truth to our own lives?

_____

_____

_____

_____

_____

WE SHOULD OBEY GOD'S TRUTH

1. Not only should we study the Scriptures and pray so that we might know God's truth, but we must also obey or walk in God's truth and rejoice when others do the same. What do the following Scriptures teach us about this truth?

   a. *II John 4*

   _____

   _____

   _____

   _____

   NOTES: The word "walk" comes from the Greek word **peripateō** [**perí** = around + **pateō** = to walk]. It is a word that is commonly used by the Apostle John to describe one's style of life or daily conduct. To walk in the truth is to order our daily lives according to God's truth, especially as it is revealed in the Scriptures.

   b. *III John 3-4*

   _____

   _____

   _____

   _____

2. In Romans 2:7-8, the righteous and their reward are contrasted with the unrighteous and their reward. Complete the following exercises with regard to these verses.

    a. *According to this passage, how important is it not only to know God's truth but also to obey it? If we are not obeying God's truth, what are we obeying? Explain your answers.*

    _____

    _____

    _____

    _____

    _____

    _____

    b. *In verse 8, the unrighteous are described both negatively (by what they do not do) and positively (by what they do). Fill in the blanks according to the text, and complete each description.*

    (1) Negatively: the unrighteous do not O_____ the T_____.

    (2) Positively: the unrighteous do O_____ U_____.

3. Our obedience to God's truth involves more than just external actions; it must include a proper inward attitude of the heart. What do the following texts teach us about this truth?

    a. *Psalm 51:6*

    _____

    _____

    _____

    _____

    NOTES: God desires that our external obedience to the truth be the result of inward truth and sincere, heartfelt loyalty to God. No other kind of obedience is acceptable.

b. *John 4:23-24*

_____

_____

_____

_____

_____

NOTES: The reference to worshiping God "in spirit" has two possible implications: (1) we must worship God sincerely and profoundly, and (2) we must worship God in the power and guidance of the Holy Spirit. The reference to worshiping God "in truth" also has two possible implications: (1) we must worship God truthfully, sincerely, and with integrity; and (2) we must worship God according to the truth—that is, according to the will of God revealed in the Scriptures.

WE SHOULD SHARE GOD'S TRUTH WITH OTHERS

1. The truth is not just for us personally, nor should **our** obedience be our only concern. If we truly love other believers and the world around us, we must share God's truth with them, that they also might live in conformity to God's will. In Psalm 40:9-10, this truth is powerfully and beautifully illustrated in the life of David. How should we imitate David's attitude and action?

_____

_____

_____

_____

2. According to the following Scriptures, what should be our attitude when seeking to share the truth of God with others?

a. *Ephesians 4:15*

_____

_____

---

b. *II Timothy 2:25*

NOTES: The word "gentleness" comes from the Greek word **praútēs**, which also denotes meekness, mildness, and forbearance. It is the very opposite of harshness and severity.

Chapter 23: God Is Faithful

The word "faithful" comes from the Hebrew word **aman** and the Greek word **pistós**. Both words communicate the idea of certainty or stability. An appropriate illustration would be a strong column that holds up the weight of a building or the strong arms of a father that uphold and protect his helpless child. When "faithful" is used with reference to God, it means that He is worthy of absolute trust and that His people can depend upon Him without doubt or reservation. It is important to understand that God's faithfulness is not based upon His doing everything that His people desire but upon His doing everything that He has promised.

1. In the Scriptures, a name is the means through which the character of a person is revealed. What names are ascribed to God in the following Scriptures?

   a. *The F_____ God (Deuteronomy 7:9).* Our God is the reliable God. He is the God who is worthy of the highest level of confidence in the matters of greatest importance to us.

   b. *The God of F_____ and without I_____ (Deuteronomy 32:4).* Faithfulness is even more than God's enduring commitment; it is an attribute of God. He is faithful; therefore, all His words and deeds are marked by faithfulness. Notice also that there is a direct relationship between God's righteousness and His faithfulness. His faithfulness flows out of His impeccable righteousness.

   c. *The H_____ One who is F_____ (Hosea 11:12).* Here we see a direct relationship between God's holiness and His faithfulness. As there is no one holy like the Lord (I Samuel 2:2), so there is no one faithful like the Lord.

   d. *The F_____ Creator (I Peter 4:19).* God's righteousness and holiness provide the moral foundation for His faithfulness. The reference to God as Creator demonstrates that He has the power necessary to fulfill every promise that He has made.

2. Our God is the faithful God, whose righteousness and power make Him infinitely more worthy than the greatest confidence that we could ever place in Him. How is God's faithfulness described in the following Scriptures? What truths are communicated?

   a. *Psalm 36:5*

   _____

   _____

   _____

   _____

NOTES: The word "faithfulness" is translated from the Hebrew word *emunah*, which denotes firmness, steadfastness, and fidelity.

b. *Psalm 100:5*

_____

_____

_____

_____

NOTES: God's faithfulness extends not only vertically to the heavens, but also horizontally throughout all generations. From the patriarchs of the Old Testament, through the disciples of the first-century Church, and even to the last saint on earth, God's faithfulness will endure undiminished.

c. *Psalm 146:5-6*

_____

_____

_____

_____

NOTES: God's continued sustaining of the earth and sea is an ever-present reminder of His enduring faithfulness to His people. The One who "upholds all things by the word of His power" (Hebrews 1:3) is able to uphold His promises to His people. We have every reason to trust and hope in Him.

3. It is important to understand that God's faithfulness not only depends upon His character, but also upon His power and immutability (*i.e.* He does not change). A god of limited power would be limited in his ability to fulfill his promises, and a mutable god could change his mind about what he has promised. What do the following Scriptures teach us about the power of the living God and His unchanging nature? Is He "able" to do all that He has promised? Will He ever change? How should the Bible's answers to these questions impact our lives?

a. *God is powerful enough to do all that He has promised.*

(1) Psalm 135:5-6

_____

_____

_____

_____

(2) Isaiah 14:24, 27

_____

_____

_____

_____

(3) Ephesians 1:11

_____

_____

_____

_____

b. *God and His promises are unchanging.*

(1) Psalm 102:25-27

_____

_____

_____

_____

(2) Malachi 3:6

_____

_____

_____

_____

NOTES: This is a powerful demonstration of how God's immutability affects His relationship with His people. Even in the midst of Israel's unfaithfulness to God, God remained faithful, because He does not change and His promises do not fail. His faithfulness to His promises does not depend upon our performance but upon His immutable and righteous character.

Chapter 24: Our Response to the Faithfulness of God

The faithfulness of God is revealed throughout all the Scriptures. There has never been one instance in all of history where God was not absolutely faithful to every word He has spoken. In the following, we will consider the implications of such faithfulness. How should we live in light of the absolute fidelity of God?

WE SHOULD TRUST IN GOD

1. In Psalm 31:14 is found one of the briefest, most powerful declarations of faith in all the Scriptures. What truths are communicated in this declaration? How should we seek to imitate the psalmist's faith?

_____

_____

_____

_____

NOTES: Two great truths are communicated in this text. First, there is a direct relationship between faith and confession—the former will lead to the latter. Second, faith involves a personal relationship. True faith requires more than a simple acknowledgment of God's existence. He must be more than **a** God or even **the** God; He must be **my** God.

2. Isaiah 26:3-4 contains both an admonition to trust in God and a promise to those who obey. Summarize each in your own words. How should both impact our lives?

   a. *The Admonition (v.4)*

_____

_____

_____

_____

NOTES: Our trust in God is to be founded upon the reality that He has revealed and proven Himself to be an everlasting Rock!

b. *The Promise (v.3)*

_____

_____

_____

_____

NOTES: Trust in God results in one of the rarest and most sought-after commodities among all of humankind—peace. Peace is a gift from God granted to those who have set their minds to trust in Him.

3. In Psalm 56:3-4 is found still another important text regarding the believer's trust in God. According to this text, how does our knowledge of God's faithfulness sustain us even in the darkest circumstances? How does our knowledge of God's faithfulness help us to persevere in the midst of trials? Is there a relationship between trust and God's Word?

_____

_____

_____

_____

4. Psalm 62:5-8 brings what we have learned to a powerful conclusion. In this text, the psalmist makes a declaration of faith and then gives us an admonition. Summarize the significance of both in your own words.

a. *The Declaration of Faith (vv.5-7)*

_____

_____

_____

_____

_____

_____

NOTES: The psalmist declares his absolute dependence upon God. God is his hope, rock, salvation, and stronghold. His hope of salvation and glory rests upon the faithfulness and power of God.

b. *The Admonition (v.8)*

_____

_____

_____

_____

WE SHOULD TRUST IN GOD'S WISDOM AND DIRECTION

1. Trust in God is not just in the mind or heart; it affects every aspect of our lives. To trust in God is to turn over the direction of our lives to Him and to be guided by His Word. What do the following texts tell us about this truth?

   a. *Psalm 37:5*

_____

_____

_____

_____

NOTES: The word "commit" comes from the Hebrew word *galal*, which literally means, "to roll." The idea is that we are to roll the entirety of our life upon the Lord. The phrase "your way" refers to the direction and activities of our lives.

b. *Proverbs 3:5-6*

_____

_____

_____

_____

_____

2. The Scriptures frequently contrast the wisdom of trusting in God with the foolishness of trusting in self. Read Jeremiah 17:5-8 until you are familiar with its contents; then describe the difference between the man who trusts in his own power and wisdom and the man who trusts in the faithfulness of God.

a. *The Man Who Trusts in Himself (vv.5-6)*

_____

_____

_____

_____

_____

b. *The Man Who Trusts in God (vv.7-8)*

_____

_____

_____

_____

_____

WE SHOULD PROCLAIM GOD'S FAITHFULNESS TO ALL

1. It is not enough that we trust in the Lord with all our heart and order our lives according to His Word; we must also share the faithfulness of God with others. What do the following Scriptures teach us about this truth?

   a. *Psalm 40:10*

   _____

   _____

   _____

   _____

   b. *Psalm 89:1*

   _____

   _____

   _____

   _____

2. It is not enough to merely affirm the truth that we should make known God's faithfulness to others, for we must actually put it into practice. We must ask ourselves whether we have proclaimed God's faithfulness to those around us or we have kept it concealed in our hearts. Based upon the above texts, explain how we might be better witnesses to the faithfulness of God.

   _____

   _____

   _____

   _____

   _____

Chapter 25: Manifestations of the Faithfulness of God

In the Scriptures are found abundant evidences of God's faithfulness to His people. If they were recorded in detail, even the world itself could not contain the books that would be written (John 21:25). However, we will limit ourselves in this chapter to a brief mention of just four manifestations or proofs of the faithfulness of God: (1) God's covenants, (2) God's word, (3) God's works, and (4) the coming of God's Son. We will consider each of these manifestations in this chapter.

THE COVENANTS OF GOD

The English word "covenant" is derived from the Latin verb *convenire* [*com* = together + *venire* = to come]. In the Scriptures, the word "covenant" comes from the Hebrew word *berit* in the Old Testament and the Greek word *diathêkē* in the New Testament. When the Bible speaks of the covenants between God and His people, it refers to the promises that God has made to His people—commitments that He has obligated Himself to fulfill without fail.

1. In Deuteronomy 7:7-9, Moses describes the covenant faithfulness of God. Summarize the truths that are revealed in this text; then explain how they apply to believers throughout all generations.

_____

_____

_____

_____

_____

_____

_____

NOTES: God's salvation and kind dealings with Israel were the result of the promises that He made to Abraham (Genesis 12:1-3) and the other patriarchs. The fact that God was still fulfilling His promises even after hundreds of years and in spite of His people's unfaithfulness is a great demonstration of His faithfulness.

2. During the dedication of the temple, King Solomon prayed a lengthy prayer extolling the faithfulness of God (I Kings 8:22-53). How does Solomon describe God and His covenant faithfulness in verses 23-24? How should Solomon's description impact our own lives?

_____

_____

_____

_____

_____

_____

_____

NOTES: Although Solomon is referring specifically to the covenant that God made with David (II Samuel 7:8-17), the same can be said of all of God's dealing with men. In all things, He has shown Himself to be a God of His word. He has not given us one reason to doubt that He will remain faithful until the end.

3. According to the following texts, how enduring is the covenant faithfulness of God? Is there any possibility that God will ever renege, default on, or fail to honor the promises that He has made to His people? Explain your answer and how it should impact our lives.

   a. *Isaiah 54:10*

   _____

   _____

   _____

   _____

   b. *Jeremiah 31:35-37; 33:20-21*

   _____

   _____

THE WORD OF GOD

The word of God (*i.e.* His promises and all that He has decreed) is another great proof of the faithfulness of God. Not one word of all the words that the Lord has spoken has ever failed. God is faithful to fulfill every promise and to carry out every decree. His word is faithful and worthy of our absolute trust because He is faithful, righteous, holy, and immutable.

1. According to Joshua 23:14, at the very end of his long life, what did Joshua testify concerning the faithfulness of God's word? How can these truths be applied to the believer's life today?

2. What do the following texts teach us about the faithfulness of God's word? How should these truths be applied to the believer's life today?

   a. *I Kings 8:56*

   b. *Psalm 119:89-90*

_____

_____

3. One of the most important truths to be emphasized about God's word is its immutability. God's word endures forever without change. What do the following texts teach us about this truth? What impact should this truth have upon our lives?

a. *Isaiah 40:7-8*

_____

_____

_____

_____

_____

b. *Matthew 5:18*

_____

_____

_____

_____

_____

THE WORKS OF GOD

It is often said that one's works verify or annul the faithfulness of one's words. When we apply this proverb to God, we find that His faithfulness is absolutely perfect. As Moses declares in Deuteronomy 32:4, "The Rock! His work is perfect."

1. In Psalm 33:4 is found a powerful declaration regarding the faithfulness of God's works. What are the truths revealed in this text, and how should they be applied to our daily lives?

_____

_____

_____

_____

_____

NOTES: It is important to recognize the relationship between God's word and His works—there is no discrepancy or variation between the two. Even among men of integrity there can be a difference between what a man says or promises and what he is actually able to perform. But God is both able and faithful to do all that He has promised!

2. In Isaiah 25:1 is found a remarkable statement about the works of God. Summarize its truths, and explain how the believer should live in light of it.

_____

_____

_____

_____

_____

NOTES: English Standard Version: "…for you have done wonderful things, plans formed of old, faithful and sure." New English Translation: "For you have done extraordinary things, and executed plans made long ago exactly as you decreed."

3. Like the texts cited above, the following Scriptures exalt the faithfulness of God's work, but with a special application to the life of every believer. What truths are communicated to us through these texts? How should they instill in us the greatest confidence?

   a. *Psalm 138:8*

_____

_____

_____

_____

b. *Philippians 1:6*

_____

_____

_____

_____

c. *I Thessalonians 5:23-24*

_____

_____

_____

_____

THE COMING OF GOD'S SON

The greatest demonstration or proof of God's faithfulness is seen in the coming of His only Son. From the very first chapters of the Scriptures, we find promises of His coming and the salvation He would bring. After thousands of years, all these promises were fulfilled in the person and work of Jesus Christ. To answer the question, "Is God faithful?" we only need to look to His Son and what He did for us on Calvary!

1. In Luke 1:46-55 is recorded what is commonly called the **Magnificat**, a prayer of Mary, the mother of Jesus. According to her words in verses 46-47 and 54-55, how has the coming of the Messiah (*i.e.* Christ) proved God's faithfulness?

_____

_____

_____

2. In Luke 1:68-79 is recorded the prophecy of Zacharias, the father of John the Baptist. According to verses 68-75, how has the coming of the Messiah proved God's faithfulness?

_____

_____

_____

_____

_____

_____

3. In Romans 15:8-9 is found one of the clearest explanations of how Christ's coming into the world is an affirmation of God's faithfulness to all men. Summarize the text and its meaning in your own words.

_____

_____

_____

_____

_____

NOTES: The word "confirmed" comes from the Greek word **bebaióō**, which means, "to confirm, secure, or establish." The sending of God's Son confirmed all the promises that He made to His people Israel. In verses 9-11, Paul makes reference to the Gentiles. Notice that Paul quotes various passages from the Old Testament where God promised to save even the Gentile nations. By sending His Son, God also confirmed all the promises He made regarding the nations.

4. In II Corinthians 1:19-20, we find one of the most beautiful and powerful texts in all the Scriptures regarding the coming of Christ. What does this text teach us? How does Christ's coming confirm God's faithfulness?

NOTES: Stated simply, all of God's promises to His people are confirmed and fulfilled in the person and work of Christ.

Chapter 26: God Is Love

LOVE – A DIVINE ATTRIBUTE

What is the love of God? It is that divine attribute that moves Him to freely and selflessly give Himself to others for their benefit or good. The Scriptures teach us that divine love (*i.e.* God's love) is much more than an attitude, an emotion, or a work. It is an ***attribute*** of God—a part of His very being or nature. God indeed loves, but He also ***is*** love. He is the very essence of what true love is, and all true love flows from Him as its ultimate source.

1. What is the name ascribed to God in II Corinthians 13:11? What does this name tell us about God's nature?

   a. *The G_____ of L_____.*

   _____

   _____

   _____

   NOTES: The truth communicated in this statement is that love is an attribute of God or an aspect of His very nature. God could no more cease to be love than He could cease to be righteous. Even in the midst of His righteous judgment, He continues to be the God of love. All of His works—even His judgment—are manifestations of His love. Finally, because God ***is*** love, He is the standard by which all other claims of love are judged.

2. In I John 4:8, 16 is found one of the most important declarations in all of the Scriptures with regard to the character and nature of God. Explain the meaning of this declaration, and describe its implications in your own words.

   _____

   _____

   _____

   _____

NOTES: Through the Apostle John, some of the greatest truths about God have been revealed to us: God is spirit (John 4:24), God is light (I John 1:5), and God is love (I John 4:8, 16). It is important to recognize that the Scriptures declare, "God is love," and not, "Love is God." The two phrases are **not** interchangeable. The universe was not created and is not ruled by a sentiment, emotion, or attitude called "love," but by the sovereign Lord of Scripture who in His very nature is love.

GOD'S RIGHTEOUS LOVE

Before we advance any further in our study of the love of God, we must make sure that we are thinking biblically and are not distorting a biblical view of God's love with the erroneous presuppositions of our contemporary culture. Modern culture has redefined love as the willingness to approve (or at least tolerate) every opinion or behavior, without judgment or censure. Any mention of an absolute standard of morality is considered narrow-minded and bigoted. Any talk of judgment or censure is seen as loveless or even hateful.

The difference between God's love and the erroneous opinion of modern man can be summarized in one word—righteousness. Righteousness is an attribute of God, an essential aspect of His nature. Thus, He cannot cease to be righteous any more than He can cease to be love. Furthermore, He cannot ignore or lay aside His righteousness, even in the name of love. God is perfect in all His ways, and all His attributes exist together in perfect harmony without contradiction or confusion. Therefore, God's love must always be a righteous love. This is the great reason for which Christ died. In Christ, God does not tolerate man's rebellion, but He confronts it and makes a way for sinful man to be reconciled to Him. He tells us that we are wrong and warns us of oncoming judgment, but He also provides a way for us to be forgiven and set right. Through the death of His Son, God satisfied the demands of His justice against sinful man, and now He can fully and freely manifest His love toward those who trust in Him.

The following summary may be helpful:

- God is love, and His love is manifested in His benevolence toward His creation, even toward sinful man.

- God is righteous, and His righteousness is manifested in the reward of the righteous and the judgment of the unrighteous.

- All men have sinned; there is no one righteous—not even one. Thus, all men are subject to the judgment of God, resulting in condemnation.

- God's love and righteousness are cooperatively manifested in the cross of Calvary. The Son of God became a man, bore the sins of men, and suffered the righteous wrath of God that was due them. By His death, He satisfied the demands of God's righteousness so that God might freely and fully manifest His love toward those who trust in Him.

– God's love is then manifested in that all who repent and trust in Christ are justified before Him and granted unbroken fellowship with Him. The righteousness of God is further manifested in that all who refuse the gospel will be judged with perfect equity and impartiality for their every thought, word, and deed.

In Exodus 34:6-7 is found one of the most important self-descriptions of God in all the Scriptures. The relationship between God's love and righteousness is also powerfully set forth in this text. Read the passage until you are familiar with its contents, and then answer the following questions.

1. In Exodus 34:6, God uses several terms to describe Himself and His disposition toward sinful men. Identify these terms. How does God describe Himself?

   a. C_____. The word is translated from the Hebrew word **rachum**, which denotes one who is compassionate or merciful, especially to the needy, weak, or sinful. It is used in Psalm 103:13 to describe the relationship between a father and his needy children: "Just as a father has compassion on his children, so the LORD has compassion on those who fear Him."

   b. G_____. The word is translated from the Hebrew word **channun**, which denotes one who shows mercy or pity to one who is in need. It is often used of a superior condescending to the needs of an inferior who has no right to make any demand. It could also be used of a creditor who has pity or mercy on a debtor who cannot pay.

   c. S_____ to A_____. The phrase may also be translated, "patient" or "longsuffering." The word "anger" comes from the Hebrew word **'af**, which literally refers to a nose or nostril. The picture communicated is that of the flaring of the nostrils, which denotes anger or wrath. The idea is not that God can tolerate sin for a long time or that it takes a great amount of sin before God becomes angry, for the Scriptures declare that God is a "God who has indignation every day" (Psalm 7:11). Rather, the idea is that God's love and mercy restrain His wrath against sinful man, giving sinners ample opportunity to repent before judgment finally falls.

   d. *Abounding in* L_____ *and* T_____. The word "lovingkindness" comes from the Hebrew word **chesed**, which is most commonly translated, "mercy," "kindness," or "lovingkindness." It can also be translated as "steadfast love" (ESV) or "loyal love" (NET). The word "truth" is translated from the Hebrew word **'emet**, which also denotes firmness or faithfulness.

2. In Exodus 34:6, we briefly considered one of the greatest self-descriptions of God in all the Scriptures—He is a God of love. According to verse 7, what is one of the implications of God's love? Explain your answer.

_____

_____

_____

NOTES: The word "forgive" comes from the Hebrew word *nasa*, which literally means, "to lift, carry, or take." The Lord is the God who takes away our sin. Three distinct terms are used to describe sin: iniquity, transgression, and sin. Although each word has a distinct meaning, the main idea being communicated is that God forgives all types of sins—sin of every kind. This truth should bring great comfort to the sinner.

3. God declares in Exodus 34:6-7 that He is the God of love and that He forgives all types and kinds of sins; however, He also explains how He will respond to those who are deemed guilty. What is this response? How can these two truths be reconciled?

_____

_____

_____

_____

_____

_____

NOTES: Here we see what seems to be a great contradiction: God loves and forgives sinful men, and yet He warns that no sinner will go unpunished. How can these two seemingly contradictory statements be reconciled? The answer is found in Jesus Christ. In His righteousness, God does punish every sinner for every sin. Yet in love, God sent His only Son as a Substitute to bear the sins of His people and suffer the punishment that was due them. In the death of Jesus Christ, God demonstrates both His justice and His love. Those who believe the gospel are freely pardoned because their sins have already been punished through the suffering and death of Christ on Calvary. Those who refuse to believe remain fully responsible for their sin and will be judged before the throne of God.

4. Based on what we have learned in this chapter, summarize in your own words the biblical truth that God's love is a righteous love.

_____

_____

_____

_____

_____

_____

5. Based on what we have learned in this chapter, summarize in your own words how the following two statements can be reconciled: (1) God forgives all types and kinds of sins; and (2) God will by no means allow the sinner to go unpunished.

_____

_____

_____

_____

_____

_____

Chapter 27: Manifestations of the Love of God

It would be easier to count all the stars in the heavens or each grain of sand on the earth than to measure or even seek to describe the love of God. Its height, depth, breadth, and width are beyond the comprehension of the greatest and most discerning creatures. Although we will never be able to fully comprehend God's love or to measure its contents, we can seek to grow in our understanding of it by considering its many demonstrations in the Scriptures.

GOD'S BENEVOLENCE TOWARD ALL CREATURES

The word "benevolence" can be defined as one's disposition to seek the "good" of others, to bless them, and to promote their welfare. It is the constant testimony of the Scriptures that God is a loving Creator who seeks the blessing and benefit of all His creatures, both the evil and the good. He is the absolute opposite of any portrayal that would depict Him as a capricious or vindictive deity who would seek the downfall and misery of His creation.

1. What do the following Scriptures teach us with regard to God's benevolence to all His creation?

   a. *Psalm 145:9, 15-16*

   _____

   _____

   _____

   _____

   _____

   b. *Matthew 5:44-45*

   _____

   _____

   _____

_____

_____

_____

c. *Acts 14:16-17*

_____

_____

_____

_____

_____

NOTES: These three examples of God's benevolence to His creation become even more astounding when we consider that creation has fallen into sin and decay. It would be an indescribable act of benevolence if the infinitely glorious God of the universe were to humble Himself to care for righteous creatures that honored Him in their every thought, word, and deed. But God shows His benevolence to fallen man, who lives in rebellion against Him.

2. According to the following Scriptures, how should all creation respond to the benevolence of God?

a. *Psalm 147:7-9*

_____

_____

_____

_____

b. *Psalm 150:6*

_____

_____

_____

_____

_____

_____

3. Considering God's benevolence to all His creation, especially to man, mankind ought to respond with praise and thanksgiving. However, according to Romans 1:21-23, how has mankind generally responded to God's benevolence?

_____

_____

_____

_____

_____

_____

NOTES: There is no greater evidence of the fallenness of man than this! Why does man reject the loving and benevolent God that he knows exists? Why does man prefer to worship self or even beasts instead of the one true God? It is because God is good, and man has become a morally depraved creature who loves unrighteousness. Therefore, he will go to the most ludicrous extremes to deny the God he knows and push Him out of his mind and conscience. But on the backdrop of man's darkness is revealed the benevolence of God, who demonstrates His love to the evil and the good (Matthew 5:44-46).

GOD'S GIVING OF HIS SON
FOR THE SALVATION OF HIS PEOPLE

We have learned that God's love is beyond comprehension and that it is manifested to all of His creatures in an almost infinite number of ways. Nevertheless, the Scriptures teach us that there is one manifestation of the love of God that rises above them all—God's giving of His only Son for the salvation of His people!

1. In I John 4:8-10 is found one of the most important passages in all of Scripture about the love of God and its greatest manifestation to men. Read the text several times until you are familiar with its contents, and then answer the following questions.

   a. *What does verse 8 teach us about the character or nature of God? Explain your answer.*

   _____

   _____

   _____

   _____

   _____

   NOTES: The truth communicated in this statement is that love is an attribute of God or an aspect of His very nature. God could no more cease to be love than He could cease to be righteous. Even in the midst of His righteous judgment, He continues to be the God of love. All of His works, even His judgments, are manifestations of His love.

   b. *According to verse 9, what is the greatest manifestation of the love of God toward His people? Explain your answer.*

   _____

   _____

   _____

   _____

   c. *According to verse 10, was God's love a response to our love for Him? Yes or no? Explain your answer.*

   _____

   _____

_____

_____

_____

NOTES: The text is very clear. Our love for God is the result of His love for us and the work of salvation that He has accomplished in our lives. It is important to note that the greatest manifestation of God's love is not just that He sent His Son (v.9), but that He sent Him to suffer and die as a propitiation. The word "propitiation" comes from the Greek word **hilasmós**, which refers to a sacrifice that is made to satisfy the demands of God's justice and make it possible for a just God to fully pardon the sinner. This is exactly what the death of Christ accomplished. It is the greatest manifestation of God's love and the greatest reason for which God's people should love Him.

2. We have learned from I John 4:8-10 that God's sending of His Son to die for the sins of His people is the greatest demonstration of unmerited and unconditional love. What do the following Scriptures teach us about this truth? Why did God send His Son to die for our sins and save us from judgment?

   a. *John 3:16-17*

   _____

   _____

   _____

   _____

   _____

   NOTES: God's love is not only manifested in God sending His Son but also in the blessing that those who believe in Him receive—eternal life. The first coming of Christ was not to judge sinners but to accomplish a work of salvation on their behalf. However, the second coming of Christ will be not only to consummate the salvation that He has begun but also to judge the unbelieving world.

   b. *Romans 5:6-8*

   _____

   _____

_____

_____

_____

NOTES: This text is packed with some of the greatest truths of Christianity. First, we learn that we were helpless to save ourselves (v.6). Second, we learn that we did not merit or deserve Christ's death on our behalf (v.7). Third, we learn that Christ's death was motivated solely by the unmerited love of God for sinners (v.8).

3. If God loved us so much that He gave His Son to die for us, even when we were "enemies" in His sight, what will this love cause Him to do for us now that we are His children? What do the following Scriptures teach us?

a. *Romans 5:8-10*

_____

_____

_____

_____

_____

NOTES: The argument of our text is flawless. (1) God's love toward His people is so great that even when we were sinners He sent His own Son to die for us. (2) Therefore, now that we have been justified by His death, we can be totally confident that we shall be saved from the wrath of God that is coming upon the entire world in the final judgment. In summation, when we were enemies, God reconciled us to Himself through the death of His Son; therefore, we can rest assured that our salvation will endure without fail through the ongoing work of His resurrected Son (Hebrews 7:25)!

b. *Romans 8:32-39*

_____

_____

_____

_____

_____

_____

c. *I John 3:1-2*

_____

_____

_____

_____

_____

_____

NOTES: Two of the greatest of all gifts that could be given to the believer are mentioned in these last two texts: (1) we will never be separated from the love of God; and (2) we will be transformed into the image of Christ.

Chapter 28: The Mercy of God

Three of the most beautiful and dearly loved concepts found in the Scriptures are the mercy, grace, and patience of God. In these three jewels, the love of God is truly manifested. In this chapter, we will consider the mercy of God.

The word "mercy" refers to the lovingkindness, tenderheartedness, or compassion of God toward even the most miserable and pitiful of His creatures. In God's mercy is found a great manifestation of His love. In many of the Scriptures given below, the idea of mercy is communicated through the words "compassion" and "lovingkindness."

1. How is God described in the following texts?

    a. *The Lord is M_____ (Psalm 145:8).* This is translated from the Hebrew word **rachum**, which also denotes kindness, lovingkindness, and compassion.

    b. *The Father of M_____ (II Corinthians 1:3).* This is translated from the Greek word **oiktirmós**, which also denotes compassion and pity. The plural possibly indicates multifaceted manifestations of mercy or all types and kinds of mercies.

    c. *The God who is R_____ in M_____ (Ephesians 2:4).* The word "rich" comes from the Greek word **ploúsios**, which may also be translated, "opulent" or "wealthy." The word "mercy" comes from the Greek word **éleos**, which also denotes pity, compassion, and kindness.

    d. *The Lord is F_____ of C_____ and is M_____ (James 5:11).* The phrase "full of compassion" is translated from a single Greek word **polúsplagchnos** [**polús** = much, many + **splágchnon** = the inward parts of the body—heart, liver, bowels, etc.]. Figuratively, it refers to deep emotions or great affections. It may also be translated, "very compassionate." The word "merciful" is translated from the Greek word **oiktírmōn**, which gives the idea that mercy is more than something God decides to do; He **is** merciful—it is essential to His nature.

2. How is God's mercy described in Psalm 57:10? What does this description mean? Write your explanation.

    _____

    _____

    _____

    _____

    _____

NOTES: The word "lovingkindness" is translated from the Hebrew word **chesed**, which may also denote mercy, kindness, favor, steadfast love (ESV), or loyal love (NET). The idea is that the lovingkindness or mercy of God is deserving of every superlative. It is bountiful, abundant, and high. It extends beyond what the most discerning eye can see, what the greatest mind can comprehend, and what the most eloquent tongue can tell.

3. According to Luke 6:35-36, how is God's mercy revealed to all men?

_____

_____

_____

_____

_____

NOTES: In this text, the relationship between love and mercy is clearly established. One of the greatest manifestations of God's love is His mercy toward undeserving and ungrateful men.

4. In Psalm 103:10-14 is recorded one of the greatest demonstrations of God's love and mercy toward His people. Read through the text several times until you are familiar with its contents, and then write your thoughts on each verse in the space below. How is God's mercy described?

   a. *Verse 10*

   _____

   _____

   _____

   _____

   b. *Verse 11*

   _____

   _____

_____

_____

NOTES: The word "lovingkindness" is translated from the Hebrew word **chesed**, which may also denote mercy, kindness, favor, "steadfast love" (ESV), or "loyal love" (NET).

c. *Verse 12*

_____

_____

_____

_____

d. *Verse 13*

_____

_____

_____

_____

NOTES: The word "compassion" is translated from the Hebrew word **rachum**, which also denotes kindness or lovingkindness.

e. *Verse 14*

_____

_____

_____

5. Although the Scriptures are filled with texts, examples, and illustrations of God's mercy, we have space for only a few more. According to the following Scriptures, how is God's mercy (lovingkindness and compassion) revealed to His people?

a. *Psalm 86:5*

_____

_____

_____

_____

b. *Lamentations 3:22-23*

_____

_____

_____

_____

6. According to the following Scriptures, how should we respond to God's mercy? How should we live in light of the biblical truth that God is merciful?

a. *Hebrews 4:16*

_____

_____

_____

_____

b. *Jude 21-22*

_____

_____

NOTES: In verses 1 and 24, Jude teaches that the believer is kept by the power of God, but here he commands the believer to keep or guard himself in the love of God. The idea is not that we are to work to earn God's love. God's love and salvation are ours only through the person and work of Christ. We keep ourselves in the love of God by clinging to Christ by faith. To depart from Christ is to step outside the sphere or realm of God's love and salvation. The idea put forth by Jude—that we are to wait anxiously for the mercy of our Lord—must be understood in its context. The believer is already a recipient of God's mercy, yet the fullness of God's mercy is yet to be revealed. That will happen at Christ's second coming and the believer's final glorification. The adverb "anxiously" does not mean that we should worry or doubt, but that we should wait earnestly and with great anticipation.

c. *Luke 6:35-36*

_____

_____

_____

_____

NOTES: This last text is concerned with our horizontal relationships (*i.e.* our relationships with other people), whether they are with believers or unbelievers. The central truth is that, since God shows mercy to undeserving sinners (including us), we should also show mercy to others. Other texts that communicate the importance of mercy in our dealings with others are Matthew 5:7; 12:7; 18:23-35.

Chapter 29: The Grace of God

The word "grace" denotes unmerited favor and refers to God's willingness to treat His creatures not according to their own merit or worth but according to His own abundant kindness and overflowing generosity. In God's grace is found a great manifestation of His love.

1. How is God described in the following texts?

   a. *The Lord is G*_____ *(Psalm 145:8).* The word is translated from the Hebrew word **channun**. This word is only used in the Scriptures as an attribute of God. Other ideas communicated by the word are: merciful, compassionate, kind, forgiving, clement, forbearing, tenderhearted, and benevolent.

   b. *The God of A*_____ *G*_____ *(I Peter 5:10).* The word is translated from the Greek word **cháris**, which denotes kindness, favor, and goodwill, especially to the undeserving. In the Scriptures, grace is God's unmerited favor to sinful man. God is the source of all grace. Every type and kind of grace—multifaceted grace, grace without measure—is found in God Himself and flows from Him.

2. According to Isaiah 30:18, what is God's attitude toward all men, especially toward His people? How can the truths of this text be applied to us? How should we respond?

_____

_____

_____

_____

_____

_____

NOTES: The context of this passage is the rebellion of God's people. They had abandoned their trust in God and entered into a sinful alliance with Egypt, yet God delayed His punishment in order to give them ample opportunity to repent and return to Him. He did this because He is not like His faithless people; He is a righteous God, who is faithful to His promises. The word "gracious" comes from the Hebrew word **chanan**, which means, "to be gracious or show favor." In the context of God's relationship with men, it is always an unmerited favor. The word "compassion" is translated from the Hebrew word **racham**, which also denotes kindness or lovingkindness.

3. According to John 1:14, 16-17, what or who is the greatest manifestation of the grace (*i.e.* unmerited favor) of God? Explain your answer.

_____

_____

_____

_____

_____

NOTES: God has manifested His grace since the fall of Adam. Even the gift of the Old Covenant Law was the result of His unmerited favor (Romans 3:1-2). However, the grace of God manifested in the person and work of Christ is so great that it eclipses all other manifestations to the degree that it is almost as though grace had never before been manifested. All other examples of God's grace are types and shadows of the fullness found in Christ. They are like the light of a candle compared to the sun shining in its noonday brightness.

4. According to the following Scriptures, what is the relationship between God's grace and the salvation of sinful men? Are we saved through our own merits or through the grace of God?

   a. *Ephesians 2:8-9*

   _____

   _____

   _____

   _____

   NOTES: In the Greek language, grace and faith are feminine gender nouns, but the pronoun "that" is neuter. Therefore, it is best to take the pronoun "that" as pointing to the fact that the entirety of our salvation is a gift from God. There is nothing of human merit in what has happened to us. Therefore, all boasting in self is eliminated.

b. *II Timothy 1:9*

_____

_____

_____

_____

_____

NOTES: God called us and saved us not because of who we are or what we have done but because He purposed in Himself to save us even before the foundation of the world. The means of saving us would not be our merit but His grace, through faith in the atoning work of Jesus Christ. In Deuteronomy 7:7-8, we find an interesting parallel. Moses declared: "The LORD did not set His love on you nor choose you because you were more in number than any of the peoples, for you were the fewest of all peoples, but because the LORD loved you...." Why did the Lord set His love upon Israel? Because He loved them! In other words, the Lord loves His people because He purposed in Himself to love us. His love for us is entirely an act of grace!

5. In the following texts from the letter to the Ephesians, the Apostle Paul sets forth God's great and eternal purpose in saving sinful men. Based upon the texts, describe this purpose in your own words.

a. *Ephesians 1:6*

_____

_____

_____

_____

NOTES: God's great purpose for saving sinful men is the manifestation of His unmerited favor, leading to the praise of His name. The word "grace" is translated from the Greek word **cháris**, which denotes favor or goodwill, especially to the undeserving; while the phrase "freely bestowed" is translated from the Greek word **charitóō**, which can also mean, "to favor or visit with favor." Notice the similarity between the words. Literally, God graced us with grace! Later, similar statements are made: "...that we who were the first to hope in Christ would be to the praise of His glory" (v.12); and "...with a view to the redemption of God's own possession, to the praise of His glory" (v.14).

b. *Ephesians 2:7*

_____

_____

_____

_____

NOTES: The manifestation of the grace of God in the believer will only increase in magnitude throughout the long ages of eternity. In fact, God's kindness toward His people in Christ Jesus will be set before all creation as the premier exhibition or demonstration of the surpassing riches of His grace. Throughout all eternity, all of creation will learn how truly gracious God is by observing His ongoing kindness toward His people. God's grace is so immense and full of wonder that even eternity will not be long enough to comprehend it or to offer Him sufficient praise for it!

6. According to the following Scriptures, how should we respond to the grace of God revealed through Jesus Christ and the gospel?

a. *Romans 6:1-2*

_____

_____

_____

NOTES: Some might conclude that, since we are saved by God's grace and not by works, it is acceptable to continue living in sin or, even worse, to increase our sinful activities so that the grace of God might become more evident. This is totally contrary to the will of God and the purpose of grace.

b. *Titus 2:11-13*

_____

_____

_____

_____

NOTES: In Romans 6:1-2, the Apostle Paul exposes a wrong and unbiblical response to God's grace. In Titus 2:11-13, he sets forth the true purpose of grace and the proper response to it.

c. *II Peter 3:18*

_____

_____

_____

_____

NOTES: God has freely bestowed His grace upon us (Ephesians 1:6). How then do we "grow" in grace as Peter commands? The idea is not that we are somehow lacking in grace and need to obtain more, but that we are to grow in the grace that has been given us in Christ. The grace of God is the sphere in which the believer now lives. Because of the grace of God manifested in the work that He has already done for us, the work He continues to do in us, the great promises He has given us, and the life and strength that He makes available to us; we can and should grow in conformity to His Son and become increasingly pleasing to Him.

d. *Hebrews 4:16*

_____

_____

_____

NOTES: God's throne of judgment (in response to our sin) has been turned into a throne of grace through the work of Christ on Calvary. It is for this reason that we can draw near with confidence. The word "confidence" is translated from the Greek word **parrhēsías** [**pás** = all + **rhêsis** = speech], which literally refers to freedom of speech and thus confidence or boldness. The greatest sinner will melt in fear before the throne of God, but the smallest saint will stand boldly and confidently because of Christ. It is in this confidence that the writer of Hebrews commands us to come to the throne of God in prayer to "find grace to help in time of need." Again, this does not mean that we are lacking in grace (Ephesians 1:6). It means that because of the grace that is ours in Christ Jesus, we should come before God and petition His help or aid in our time of need. Though all that we need is already ours, it must often be appropriated through believing and persevering in prayer to God. Oftentimes, we do not have the help we need because we do not ask (James 4:2).

e. *Acts 20:24*

_____

_____

_____

_____

NOTES: This was the Apostle Paul's noble goal. Although our callings, gifts, and ministries may be different from his, we should all have this same ambition—to testify of the gospel of the grace of God.

Chapter 30: The Patience of God

The words "patience" and "longsuffering" refer to God's willingness to bear with or suffer long with the weakness and wrongdoing of His creatures. In God's patience is found a great manifestation of His love, especially in light of the sinfulness of mankind. God deserves all glory, honor, and praise. The fact that He bears with men who render unto Him the very opposite of what He deserves is a great demonstration of His enduring and patient love.

1. In Exodus 34:6-7 is found one of the greatest revelations of God in the Old Testament. In this text, God comes down and allows His glory to pass by Moses. In the midst of this great event, God declares many essential truths about Himself and about His relationship with man. In verse 6, what does God declare to Moses and us about His patience or longsuffering?

   a. *The Lord is S_____ to A_____.*

      NOTES: This declaration is also found in Numbers 14:18; Nehemiah 9:17; Psalm 86:15; 103:8; 145:8; Joel 2:13; Jonah 4:2; and Nahum 1:3. The frequency with which this description of God occurs in the Scriptures demonstrates both its importance and truthfulness—God really is patient! The word "anger" comes from the Hebrew word *'af*, which literally means, "nose" or "nostril." The flaring of the nostrils symbolizes anger or wrath. The Scriptures teach that God is a consuming fire (Deuteronomy 4:24; Hebrews 12:29) and that His wrath can quickly ignite (Psalm 2:12 NET). However, the quick kindling of His anger comes only after His great patience has run its course. These promises serve as a reminder that although God is slow to anger, we must not presume upon His patience or put the Lord our God to the test.

2. According to I Peter 3:20, why did God delay so long before judging the world in the days of Noah? What attribute of God caused Him to hold back His hand of judgment? What does this teach us about God's nature?

   _____

   _____

   _____

   _____

   NOTES: The word "patience" comes from the Greek word **makrothumía** [**makrós** = long + **thumós** = passion, anger, outbursts of anger] and denotes longsuffering or endurance. The phrase "kept waiting" properly translates the imperfect Greek verb—God waited and waited for the people to repent. In fact, during the entire 120 years that Noah built the ark, God endured with great patience man's wickedness and gave him ample opportunity to repent.

3. The patience or longsuffering of God is especially manifested in the kindness that He showed the nation of Israel. A powerful example of this truth is found in Psalm 78:36-42. Read the text several times until you are familiar with its contents, and then answer the following questions.

a. *According to verses 36-37, how did the nation of Israel respond to God's gracious dealings with them?*

_____

_____

_____

_____

NOTES: This passage lays out three great sins of the Israelites. First, their hearts were not "steadfast" toward God. This comes from the Hebrew word *kun*, which means, "to be firm or established." They were unstable in their love and loyalty to God. Second, they deceived or lied to God with their words—this is probably a reference to the broken vows they had made, their superficial repentance, and their hypocrisy in worship. Third, they were not faithful to God's covenant. God's covenant with Israel was two-sided. God remained faithful to all His promises, but Israel was neglectful and disobedient to God's law.

b. *According to verses 40-42, what else did the Israelites do in response to God's gracious dealings with them?*

_____

_____

_____

_____

NOTES: Five more sins are added to Israel's account. First, they rebelled against God. The word is translated from the Hebrew word **marah**, which also means, "to be contentious." Secondly, they grieved God. The word is translated from the Hebrew word **atsab**, which means, "to pain or to hurt." Thirdly, they tempted God. The word is translated from the Hebrew word **nasah**. It is the same word used in Deuteronomy 6:16: "You shall not put the Lord your God to the test." Fourthly, they pained God. The word is translated from the Hebrew word **tawah**, which also means, "to wound." Finally, they forgot God, followed after idols, and did what was right in their own eyes. These sins, along with those mentioned in verses 36-37, summarize Israel's apostasy against God.

c. *According to verses 38-39, how did God respond to Israel's almost constant rebellion?*

_____

_____

_____

_____

_____

NOTES: God's response to Israel's rebellion is here summarized. First, He was compassionate toward them (v.38). Second, He forgave their iniquity (v.38). Third, He restrained His anger (v.38). Fourth, He pitied them, remembering that they were but fallen men (v.39).

d. *In your own words, describe what God's response teaches us about His patience or longsuffering? How should we apply these truths to our own lives?*

_____

_____

_____

_____

_____

4. What is the motivation behind God's patience toward even the greatest of sinners? Why is He so patient, so willing to bear with disobedient and ungrateful humanity? What do the following Scriptures teach us?

a. *Ezekiel 18:23, 32*

_____

_____

_____

_____

b. *II Peter 3:9*

_____

_____

_____

_____

5. According to Romans 2:4, how should men respond to God's patience and longsuffering toward their sin? What should the sinner do in light of God's kindness?

_____

_____

_____

_____

NOTES: God is here said to be rich in three things: (1) kindness—from the Greek word **chrēstótēs**, which also denotes benevolence, goodness, and gentleness; (2) tolerance—from the Greek word **anochê**, which denotes forbearance, endurance, and a willingness to delay; and (3) patience—from the Greek word **makrothumía**, which denotes longsuffering and endurance. All of these qualities should melt the sinner's hardened heart and lead him to repentance.

Chapter 31: God Is the Creator

GOD THE CREATOR

One of the foundational truths of Scripture and the Christian faith is that God is the Creator of the heavens and the earth. He is before all things, and all things exist because of Him. He was not caused or made by something or someone greater than Himself; rather, He is the Cause and Maker of all things, and nothing that does exist would exist apart from Him. He alone is Creator; no one shares this title with Him.

The belief that God created all beings in heaven and on earth should radically affect every aspect of our lives. **First**, it should lead to awe and reverence. The knowledge that there is a God so great that He has created innumerable worlds and beings and sustains them effortlessly is beyond comprehension. Such a God is worthy of absolute reverence. If at times we stand in awe of His creation, how much more should we stand in awe of Him? **Secondly**, it should lead to thanksgiving and worship. If God had not created us, we would not be. To refuse Him thanksgiving and praise is to be guilty of the greatest arrogance and ingratitude. **Thirdly**, it should lead to humility. What is man that God should take thought of him? We exist because He made us, and apart from Him we are nothing. A lack of humility before God is beyond comprehension. **Fourthly**, it should give purpose to our existence. We are not the result of random chance or some mindless process of naturalistic evolution. We were made according to God's design and for His purpose and good pleasure.

1. In the Scriptures, a person's name has great significance in that it often describes who he is and reveals something about his character. What is the name given to God in Isaiah 40:28? What does it teach us about His greatness? What should it mean to His people?

   _____

   _____

   _____

   _____

2. Some of the most important statements in Scripture with regard to God as Creator are found in the following passages. Consider carefully each verse, and identify the truths that are being communicated. What do they teach us about God? What do they teach us about man's dependence and indebtedness to God?

   a. *Genesis 1:1-2*

   _____

   _____

_____

_____

NOTES: In this context, "beginning" refers to the inauguration of the creation of the universe. It comes forth from God and thus presupposes God's eternality. The word "created" comes from the Hebrew word **bara**, which in the Scriptures is used only with reference to God. Not even the highest order of angels contributed to creation; it is the product of God's design alone. Thus, all glory belongs to God alone!

b. *Nehemiah 9:6*

_____

_____

_____

_____

NOTES: This text is an affirmation of Genesis 1:1-2. Creation is the work of God alone, and to Him alone is worship due. If the heavenly hosts bow down before God because of creative work, how much more should mortal man bow in reverence, worship, and thanksgiving?

c. *Jeremiah 10:12*

_____

_____

_____

_____

NOTES: It is important to note that the creation reveals something not only of the power of God, but also of His wisdom. The power needed to create and sustain the world is incalculable, but God brings it to pass without the slightest reduction of His power or strength. Similarly, the complexity of the smallest cell baffles the most brilliant of men, but the creation of the entire universe is only a small example of God's wisdom and understanding.

d. *Hebrews 11:3*

_____

_____

_____

_____

NOTES: Theologians often use a Latin phrase to describe God's work of creation: ***creatio ex nihilo***—creation out of nothing. God did not use already existing materials to make the universe; He created it out of nothing, by His own power, and for His own glory.

3. It is important to understand that the creation of the universe was the work of the Triune God—Father, Son, and Spirit. What do the following texts teach us about this truth? What do they add to our understanding of God as Creator and Sustainer of the universe?

a. *Genesis 1:1-2*

_____

_____

_____

_____

NOTES: The word "Spirit" comes from the Hebrew word ***ruach***, which may also be translated, "breath" or "wind." The word "moving" is translated from the Hebrew word ***rachaf***, which means, "to hover." Some modern interpreters have argued that a reference is being made to the wind rather than the personal Spirit; however, such an interpretation does not fit the context. The wind does not hover. The text clearly refers to the creative work of the Person of the Holy Spirit.

b. *John 1:1-3*

_____

_____

_____

_____

> **NOTES:** Verse 1 makes it clear that the subject of our text is the Word, the Son of God. John's language could not be more emphatic. All things that exist, without exception, came into being through the creative work of the Son.

c. *Colossians 1:16*

_____

_____

_____

_____

> **NOTES:** The three phrases "by Him," "through Him," and "for Him" (literally, **eis autón** or "unto Him") are extremely important. The Son is not only the Agent of creation, but He is also the purpose or goal of creation. Both truths are clear affirmations of the Son's deity. All things were made by the Son and for His honor and good pleasure.

CREATION'S WITNESS TO GOD

Naturalistic evolution seeks to explain creation apart from the existence of God. Although the theory is the predominant thought of our day, it is contrary to everything that reason and the Scriptures declare about our existence. We should never attempt to create a false truce between evolution and the biblical view of the Creator God. If evolution is true, then the Bible is a lie. If the Bible is true, then evolution is nothing more than man's pathetic attempt to deny the God who he knows exists. The purpose of this brief section is not to debate evolution, but to simply put forth the truths of the Scriptures regarding the universe as the creation of God.

1. According to Psalm 19:1-4, how does creation bear witness to the existence, power, and glory of God? Summarize the truths revealed in this text.

_____

_____

_____

_____

_____

NOTES: Although creation has no voice, its beauties and complexities declare the existence and glory of God. The phrase, "their line has gone out," is difficult to interpret. The alternative translation, "their sound [or voice] has gone out" is preferable. It is also the interpretation found in the Septuagint (the ancient Greek translation of the Old Testament).

2. In Hebrews 3:4 is a very important analogy that can be applied to the creation of the universe. How does an ordered and complex universe prove the existence of God?

_____

_____

_____

_____

_____

_____

NOTES: It would be absurd to think that the house in which a person lives simply came into being by means of random events. The existence of a house with design implies a builder with intelligence. How much more do the complexities and intricate design of the universe demand a personal and purposeful Creator of infinite wisdom?

3. Romans 1:18-23 is one of the most important texts in all the Scriptures regarding God's existence, the creation of the universe, and man's knowledge of God. Read through the text several times until you are familiar with its contents, and then answer the following questions.

   a. *What does Romans 1:19-20 testify about the knowledge of God? Has enough evidence been given to all men that they can rightly be held accountable? Explain your answer.*

_____

_____

_____

_____

_____

NOTES: The Scriptures do not acknowledge or recognize the existence of atheists. It boldly declares that all men know that there is a God of eternal power who is the only plausible explanation for the universe. This truth is affirmed in Romans 1:21: "For even though they knew God...." Some scholars believe that Paul is describing two sources of the knowledge of God. First, there is an internal, innate, or inherent knowledge of God in every man—"that which is known about God is evident within them" (v.19). Second, there is a knowledge of God that comes from examining creation (v.20). The latter confirms the former.

b. *According to Romans 1:21, how has mankind in general responded to the knowledge of God?*

   (1) They did not H_____ Him as God. From the Greek word **doxázō**, which literally means, "to glorify" or "to esteem as glorious." The term may also communicate the idea of extolling, magnifying, or worshiping God. Man's refusal to acknowledge God makes it impossible for them to glorify or honor Him. Further offense is committed by attributing the wonders of His creation to a mindless process of random chance. Paul's declaration here possibly gives us insight into the meaning of Romans 3:23—"for all have sinned and fall short of the glory of God." That is, all have fallen short of giving God the glory or honor that is due Him.

   (2) They did not give T_____. In Acts 17, Paul declares to the Athenians, "He Himself gives to all people life and breath and all things" (v.25), and "in Him we live and move and exist" (v.28). For this reason, man's ingratitude to God is an offense of the most grotesque sort.

c. *According to Romans 1:21-23, what has been the result of man's rejection of God?*

   _____

   _____

   _____

   _____

   _____

NOTES: This text reads like the history of man—a history of futile speculation, foolishness, moral and intellectual darkness, pride, arrogance, and idolatry. The moral, emotional, psychological, spiritual, and sociological maladies that plague man are the result of his rejection of God.

d. *According to Romans 1:18, what is the primary reason for man's rejection of God as Creator of the universe? Is the problem intellectual or moral?*

_____

_____

_____

_____

_____

NOTES: The word "ungodliness" comes from the Greek word *asébeia*, which denotes a lack of reverence for God. The word "unrighteousness" comes from the Greek word *adikía*, which denotes lack of conformity to the will of God. The word "suppress" comes from the Greek word *katéchō*, which means, "to hold fast or hold back; to hinder, restrain, or detain." Thus, the primary reason for man's rejection of God is moral. Fallen man is unrighteous and does not desire a righteous God. Therefore, he suppresses the truth he knows about God and strives to convince himself that God does not exist.

KNOWING THE LIVING GOD

Chapter 32: God Is the Sustainer and Owner of Creation

GOD THE SUSTAINER

The Scriptures teach us that God is not only the Creator but also the Sustainer of the heavens and the earth. Nothing that exists would exist apart from Him. If He were to turn away from His creation for even a moment, all would perish. We owe our every breath and movement to Him. Every being—from the highest angel to the lowest worm—lives in absolute dependence upon God. Both the man who bows in humble worship and he who clenches his fist in defiance of God have this in common—they live and breathe and move by His gracious, sustaining power. They exist because He made them, and they breathe because He gives them breath. If He turned away from them, they would turn to dust.

1. In I Timothy 6:13 is found a very brief but powerful declaration about God and about creation's dependence upon Him. Identify the declaration, and then explain its meaning.

   a. *God gives L_____ to all T_____.*

   b. *What does this declaration teach us about God's power and about creation's absolute dependence upon Him?*

   _____

   _____

   _____

   _____

2. The Scriptures teach us not only that God created the universe, but also that He faithfully sustains it by His power. Without God, the universe would never have been brought into existence; and without His continued care, the universe and every living thing would perish. All things that exist do so in absolute dependence upon Him. What do the following Scriptures teach us about this great truth?

   a. *Job 12:10*

   _____

   _____

_____

_____

b. *Job 34:14-15*

_____

_____

_____

_____

c. *Psalm 104:27-30*

_____

_____

_____

_____

3. It is important to understand that not only the creation but also the sustaining of the universe is the work of the Triune God—Father, Son, and Spirit. What do the following texts teach us about this truth? What do they add to our understanding of God as Creator and Sustainer of the universe?

    a. *Colossians 1:17*

    _____

    _____

    _____

    _____

    NOTES: The phrase "hold together" comes from the single Greek verb **sunístēmi**, [*sún* = with, together + **hístēmi** = to stand], which can also mean, "to unite, set together, or endure." The Son of God is not only the Creator of all things but also the Sustainer or Conserver of all that He has created. As the divine **Logos** or Word (John 1:1-5), He is the unifying principle of all that exists. From the greatest galaxies to the tiniest particles, everything is held together in the Son.

b. *Hebrews 1:3*

_____

_____

_____

_____

NOTES: The word "upholds" comes from the Greek verb *phérō*, which means, "to bear or carry." We marvel at the idea of mighty Atlas of Greek mythology groaning under the weight of the world. Yet Christ upholds the entire universe with a mere word—a simple, effortless command. With a word the universe was created (Genesis 1:3; Hebrews 11:3), and with a word it is sustained. Such is the power of God.

c. *Psalm 104:27-30*

_____

_____

_____

_____

NOTES: In verse 30, creation is seen as an ongoing work of God by the power of His Spirit. Even though the birth of a child is through natural processes, it is not apart from the work of God. In Psalm 139:13, David testified, "For You formed my inward parts; You wove me in my mother's womb." It is through the powerful, energizing, life-giving work of the Spirit that the sustaining work of the Father and Son is accomplished.

4. In Acts 17:22-31 is recorded the Apostle Paul's sermon to the Epicurean and Stoic philosophers on Mars Hill. The passage contains one of the greatest discourses on God as both the Creator and Sustainer of the universe. According to the following verses, complete the four great declarations that are made about God and about man's absolute dependence upon Him; then explain their meanings.

a. *He is the God who made the W_____ and all T_____ in it (v.24).*

_____

_____

_____

_____

NOTES: The Apostle Paul first establishes God as the Creator of all things. This is the foundation of God's claim upon creation.

b. *He is the Lord of H_____ and E_____ (v.24).*

_____

_____

_____

_____

NOTES: As the Creator of all things, God has the sovereign right to rule over all things.

c. *He gives to all people L_____ and B_____ and A_____ things (v.25).*

_____

_____

_____

_____

NOTES: God has a claim upon all things both by right of creation and by right of His benevolent sustaining of all that He has made. Every breath, every beat of every heart, and "every good thing given" are all from God (James 1:17). In light of God's benevolent giving and man's absolute dependence upon Him, man's ingratitude is inexcusable.

d. *In Him we L_____, M_____, and E_____ (v.28).*

_____

_____

_____

_____

NOTES: This quote is likely taken from a poem attributed to Epimenides of Crete (c. 600 B.C.), which relates the hymn of Minos (a figure of Greek mythology) to his father Zeus. It is interesting to note that just two lines earlier in the hymn is found the quote which Paul uses in Titus 1:12: "Cretans are always liars, evil beasts, lazy gluttons." Although Paul is using a declaration from the Greek poets, he is not endorsing their polytheistic ideas; he is simply using their own language to point them away from what they worshiped "in ignorance" (v.23) to the true and living God of the Scriptures.

GOD THE OWNER OF ALL

God is the Creator and Sustainer of all things in heaven and on earth. Therefore, it is not wrong that He claims all things as His own. One of the "first truths" that must be comprehended if we are to have a right understanding of God and our place in His creation is that we are not our own. We were not made for ourselves. We belong to the One who made us, and we are responsible before Him to live according to His will and for His glory and good pleasure.

1. In the Scriptures, a person's name has great significance in that it often describes who he is and reveals something about his character. What is the name given to God in Genesis 14:19, 22? What truth does it communicate to us about Him?

_____

_____

_____

_____

_____

NOTES: The word "possessor" comes from the Hebrew word **qanah**, which means, "to get or acquire," and is used of God to communicate that He is both the Creator and the Possessor of the universe.

2. The following passages contain two of the most important statements in all the Scriptures with regard to God's ownership of His creation. Consider carefully each verse, and then identify the truths that are being communicated. How do they demonstrate God's claim upon creation, especially upon mankind? How should we respond?

a. *Psalm 24:1-2*

_____

_____

_____

_____

b. *Psalm 89:11*

_____

_____

_____

_____

3. The following texts from Job and Psalms communicate to us a very important implication of God's ownership of creation. Consider each text, and write your thoughts. How should we live in response to the truth that is taught in these texts?

a. *Job 41:11*

_____

_____

_____

_____

b. *Psalm 50:10-12*

_____

_____

_____

_____

_____

NOTES: The great truth communicated in both of these texts is that, because He is the Creator and Sustainer of all, God needs nothing from man and is debtor to no man. Everything that we may offer Him originated with Him and is His. God does not call us to serve Him because of some need, but in order that we might know the privilege of His fellowship and witness the demonstration of His power.

4. In Deuteronomy 10:14-15, we discover both the greatness of God with regard to His creation and the grace of God to His people. Consider the text, and write your thoughts.

_____

_____

_____

_____

NOTES: One of the most amazing truths communicated to us in these two verses is the grandeur of God as the Owner of all creation and His amazing grace toward His people. It is truly amazing that a God so great would set His affections upon us and love us.

Chapter 33: The Purpose of Creation

We have learned from the Scripture that God is the Creator, Sustainer, and rightful Owner of His creation. It now follows that we consider the purpose for which He created all things. If God was under no obligation to create the universe, and if He did not need the universe to fill some void in His existence, then what was and is the divine purpose behind the creation and continued existence of man? The Scriptures boldly and unapologetically declare creation's purpose to be *the glory and good pleasure of God*.

THE GOD OF ALL FULLNESS

One of the most awe-inspiring and humbling truths about God is that He is absolutely free from any need or dependence. His existence, the fulfillment of His will, and His happiness or good pleasure do not depend upon anyone or anything outside of Himself. As we learned in Chapter Eleven, He is the only Being who is truly self-existent, self-sustaining, self-sufficient, independent, and free. All other beings derive their life and blessedness from God, but all that is necessary for God's existence and perfect happiness is found in Himself. To even suggest that God made man because He was lonely or incomplete is absurd and even blasphemous. Creation is not the result of some lack in God, but the result of His fullness or the overflow of His abundance.

1. What do the following Scriptures teach us about the self-existence and self-sufficiency of God? From where does God's life or existence come? Is He dependent upon another?

   a. *Psalm 36:9*

   _____

   _____

   _____

   _____

   _____

   b. *John 5:26*

   _____

   _____

   _____

_____

_____

NOTES: God has life in Himself and is the fountain of life and light (*i.e.* wisdom) for all living creatures. He is not dependent upon another; all things are dependent upon Him.

2. The self-sufficiency of God is a declaration of His infinite greatness and His exalted place above His creation. All things depend upon Him for their very existence, but He depends upon no one. In Acts 17:22-31 is recorded the Apostle Paul's sermon to the Epicurean and Stoic philosophers on Mars Hill. In verses 24-25, he refutes their idolatrous views by making two very important declarations about the living God. What do these declarations teach us about God's self-sufficiency and His relationship to His creation?

a. *God does not dwell in temples made with hands (v.24).*

_____

_____

_____

_____

_____

b. *God is not served by human hands as though He had need (v.25).*

_____

_____

_____

_____

_____

NOTES: The first declaration proves that God has no need that man should build Him a temple, since He Himself made the universe, and even it cannot contain Him. The second declaration proves that God's command for us to serve Him is not the result of need on His part; it is an act of grace. He grants us the privilege of knowing Him, serving Him, and being the special objects of His favor.

THE GLORY OF GOD

If God did not create the universe because of some need, then what was His purpose? Why did God create all things? The Scriptures teach us that God created everything for His own good pleasure and glory (*i.e.* to manifest His greatness and to receive from His creation the honor and worship that is due Him). This may sound strange or even a bit self-centered and self-ish on God's part, but nothing could be further from the truth. Consider these two evidences. **First**, God is worthy to take the highest place above His creation; and He is worthy to be the object of all our thoughts, activities, and worship. For Him to deny Himself "first place" above us would be for Him to deny that He is God. **Secondly**, the greatest good God could ever do for us and the greatest kindness He could ever show us would be to direct all things so that His greatness might be fully displayed before us. If God is of infinite worth, beauty, and majesty, then the most valuable, beautiful, and majestic gift He could ever give us would be to show us His glory.

1. God is the Creator, Sustainer, and rightful Owner of the heavens and the earth and all that dwells within them. All things were **created by** Him, **belong to** Him, and **exist for** His glory. What does Romans 11:36 teach us about this truth? Complete each statement.

   a. *F_____ Him are all things.* God is the **source** of creation and the fountain of all life (Psalm 36:9). Creation owes its very existence to God, and apart from Him there would be nothing. Man is not the product of some mindless evolutionary process that he should live without purpose; nor is he the source of his own existence that he should live for himself; rather, he is the work of God that he should live for His glory.

   b. *T_____ Him are all things.* God is the **Agent** through which all things were created and are sustained. If God were to turn away from His creation for one moment, all would become **chaos**. But through His unhindered sovereignty, un-searchable wisdom, and infinite power, He sustains all things and directs them (mole-cules, men, and galaxies) to the great end for which they were created—the glory of God.

   c. *T_____ Him are all things.* In this simple phrase is found the meaning of existence. God created all things and works in all things for His good pleasure and glory—to manifest His greatness and receive from us the honor and worship that are due Him.

   d. *T_____ Him be the G_____ forever. A_____.* The only proper re-sponse to the greatness of God is to esteem Him above all things and to give to Him the highest honor, adoration, and praise. There is an important Latin phrase used in theology to describe this truth—**soli Deo gloria**, which means, "to God alone be the glory."

2. In Colossians 1:16 is found a passage of Scripture that is very similar to Romans 11:36, but it speaks specifically about the Son of God. What does this text teach us about the purpose of creation?

   a. *All things have been created B_____ Him and T_____ Him.* The Father is the source of all things (Romans 11:36), but He has created all things **through** the Son

(John 1:3; Hebrews 1:2), who is the Mediator between the Father and creation. Through the Son, the Father **created** all things, **reveals** Himself to His creation (John 1:18), **reconciled** the creation to Himself (II Corinthians 5:19), **rules** creation (Philippians 2:9-11), and will one day **judge** creation (John 5:22).

b. *All things have been created F_____ Him.* It is no contradiction to say that all things have been created for the glory and good pleasure of both the Father and the Son. According to the Scriptures, the Father loves the Son and has given all things into His hand (John 3:35). And it is the Father's will that all honor the Son as they honor Him (John 5:23). Therefore, everything said in Romans 11:36 about the purpose of creation may also be applied to the Son. All creation, in all realms, has one great and final purpose—the glory of God.

Chapter 34: Our Response to God as the Creator

REVERENCE AND HUMILITY

Our first response to God as Creator should be one of reverence and humility. We reverence God to the degree that we acknowledge His highest place before us as Creator and Lord of all and regard Him with the utmost respect and awe. We humble ourselves to the degree that we acknowledge our place before Him as creatures—His possession, created for His glory and good pleasure. When men correctly understand creation's relationship to the Creator, they lay prostrate before God with reverence, trembling, and a real sense of utter dependence upon the One who made them.

1. In light of the awesome power and grandeur of God, mankind's first response should be that of reverence and awe. Read Psalm 33:6-9. According to verse 8, how should the inhabitants of earth respond to the infinite power and wisdom of God revealed through creation?

NOTES: The word "fear" is translated from the Hebrew word **yare**. With respect to God, it denotes having the greatest reverence for who He is, what He has done, and what He can do. The word "awe" is translated from the Hebrew word **gur**, which also denotes fear or dread. God is not to be feared because of some inconsistency or immorality in His person or works. Rather, it is the unchanging uprightness of God—His righteousness, holiness, majesty, and power—that calls for our reverence.

2. Awe and reverence are inseparable from humility. If we have truly comprehended something of the infinite perfections and power of God, we will humble ourselves before Him. Read Psalm 8:1-4. According to verse 4, how did the psalmist's contemplation of God's creation

produce in him an attitude of great humility? How should this attitude also be reflected in the life of every man?

_____

_____

_____

_____

WORSHIP AND ADORATION

How can the creature not worship its Creator and Sustainer? The debt that is owed Him cannot be measured. Would anything exist if He had not spoken? Would not all things immediately turn to chaos and destruction if He did not sustain them? Could the constellations and planets find their way without Him? Would not the seas escape their boundaries and engulf the land if His hand did not hold them back? Could man draw even one more breath were it not granted to him by God? How then can we not worship? It would not be wrong to say that the primary purpose of creation, especially of man, is to worship the God who created us and by whose power and faithfulness we are sustained. The worship of God is our highest privilege and greatest responsibility. When we do worship Him, we are at last fulfilling the purpose for which we were created.

1. According to Revelation 4:11, why is God worthy to be praised?

_____

_____

_____

_____

NOTES: The adjective "worthy" comes from the Greek word **áxios**, which denotes something or someone of weight or great worth. God is deserving of all praise, thanksgiving, and service.

2. In Psalm 148:1-13 is found a call for all creatures of every realm to render worship, honor, and glory to the God who made them. Read the text until you are familiar with its contents, and then complete the following exercises.

a. *Identify the different creatures and realms of creation that are called to offer worship to God.*

_____

_____

_____

_____

NOTES: The purpose of this exercise is to demonstrate that there is simply not enough time or space to list all the different creatures that owe praise to God. If even beasts and creeping things owe praise to Him, how much more does man, who has been given grace, position, and privilege above all?

b. *According to verses 5-6, why is creation called to offer praise to God?*

_____

_____

_____

_____

NOTES: According to verse 6, God has established the natural order of His creation, and this order is fixed under His sovereign decree. Nothing will happen except that which is part of His government or rule. No catastrophe will come upon the world except that which has been decreed by God.

c. *According to verse 13, why is creation called to offer praise to God?*

_____

_____

_____

NOTES: God's creation is a thing of indescribable glory, yet it does not begin to compare with the infinite glory of God's person. He is to be praised not only (or even primarily) for what He has done, but also for who He is.

3. We will conclude our study of God as Creator and Sustainer with two commands that reach to every realm and every inhabitant of creation. What is commanded? How shall we live in light of these commands?

a. *Psalm 103:22*

_____

_____

_____

_____

NOTES: The word "bless" comes from the Hebrew word **barak**, which is often used in the Scriptures to denote a joyous and exuberant exclamation of praise and thanksgiving to God.

b. *Psalm 150:6*

_____

_____

_____

_____

NOTES: The word "praise" is translated from the Hebrew word **halal**, which means, "praise." The title "Lord" is translated from the Hebrew word **yhwh** or **yah**, which is transliterated as "Yahweh." It is from these two words that we derive the term "hallelujah." In Hebrew, repetition (as throughout this psalm) is extremely important; it is intended to communicate emphasis or intensity.

Chapter 35: God Is the Lord and Sovereign over All

The Scriptures teach us not only that God is the Creator and Sustainer of the universe, but also that He is its Sovereign Lord and King. He rules over all creatures, actions, and things—from the greatest to the smallest—by His perfect wisdom, infinite power, and absolute righteousness. He is free to do all things according to His own will and to do them for His own glory and good pleasure. No power in heaven or on earth can annul what He has determined.

THE SUPREMACY OF GOD

Before we explore the details of His sovereignty, we must first consider a doctrine that is absolutely essential to a correct understanding of God—His supremacy. The word "supreme" refers to that which is highest in excellence, rank, or authority. The **supremacy of God** refers to His exalted place above all creation.

The truth of God's supremacy has many important implications. With regard to **God's person**, it means that He is infinitely more excellent than any of His creatures and of infinitely greater worth than all of His creation combined. With regard to **God's place**, it means that He is exalted above all creation and has no equals. With regard to **God's purpose**, it means that He is at the very center of all things and that He directs all things toward one great goal—His own glory.

1. In the Scriptures, a name has great significance in that it often describes who a person is and reveals something about his or her character. What are the names or titles ascribed to God in the following Scriptures? What do they reveal to us about His supremacy and His relationship to His creation, especially to man?

   a. *Psalm 97:9*

   _____

   _____

   _____

   _____

NOTES: The name, "Lord Most High," is translated from the Hebrew phrase **Yahweh-Elyon**, which communicates the sovereignty, exaltation, and majesty of Yahweh (see also Psalm 7:17 and Psalm 47:2). This Scripture is not teaching that there is more than one true God. In the time of the psalmist (as well as today), the nations were inundated with false gods and the worship of idols. The Apostle Paul states that these so-called gods were nothing more than demons and that those who sacrificed to them sacrificed to demons (I Corinthians 10:20; see also Leviticus 17:7; Deuteronomy 32:17; Psalm 106:37). Psalm 97:9 is simply stating that God is exalted and sovereign over all things—including the false idols of men and the powerful demonic influences behind them.

b. *Isaiah 57:15*

_____

_____

_____

_____

NOTES: The phrases, "the high and exalted One" and "whose name is Holy," both communicate the same truth about God. The word "holy" comes from the Hebrew word **qadosh**, which means, "separated, marked off, placed apart, or withdrawn from common use." With regard to God, the word has at least two important meanings: (1) God is transcendent above His creation, and (2) He is transcendent above His creation's corruption.

2. Having considered the divine names that reveal God's supremacy, we will now consider one of the most beautiful declarations of the supremacy of God in the Scriptures. Read I Chronicles 29:11 until you are familiar with its contents, and then answer the following questions.

a. *What are the six attributes and rights that are ascribed to God?*

(1) G_____. From the Hebrew word **gedolah**. God's greatness is an eternal and immutable attribute, not merely a title that He has earned. He always has been and always will be infinitely greater than anything to which He is compared.

(2) P_____. From the Hebrew word **gevurah**, which also denotes strength and might. In the realm of power, there is no one who can contend with God. If all the forces of creation were to come together in a single army to oppose the throne of God, it would be as pointless and unthreatening as a tiny gnat pounding its head against a world of granite.

(3) G_____. From the Hebrew word **tif'arah**, which also denotes beauty. It is often used to describe the splendor of garments or the magnificence of jewels. The most breathtaking beauty of creation is a dark shadow compared to the One who created all.

(4) V_____. From the Hebrew word **netzach**, which can communicate different meanings depending on the context. In one context, it may communicate

victory or strength; but in another, it can communicate the idea that something or someone is perpetual or enduring.

(5) M_____. From the Hebrew word **hod**, which may also denote splendor, honor, beauty, or vigor.

(6) D_____. From the Hebrew word **mamlakhah**, which communicates ideas of kingdom, sovereignty, reign, and rule. The pagan king Nebuchadnezzar declared of God, "His dominion is an everlasting dominion, and His kingdom endures from generation to generation. All the inhabitants of the earth are accounted as nothing, but He does according to His will in the host of heaven and among the inhabitants of earth; and no one can ward off His hand or say to Him, 'What have You done?'" (Daniel 4:34-35).

b. *Explain in your own words how these six attributes demonstrate God's supremacy over all.*

_____

_____

_____

_____

_____

_____

c. *Having declared the greatness and supremacy of God over all things, I Chronicles 29:11 concludes with a very important statement about God. What does God do for Himself? What does this communicate to us about God and His supremacy over all things?*

_____

_____

_____

_____

_____

_____

_____

NOTES: Why is it right for God to exalt Himself as head over all? The answer is two-fold. First, God is the most worthy Being to take the highest place above His creation. For Him to deny Himself "first place" above us would be to deny that He is God. Second, the greatest good God could ever do for us and the greatest kindness He could ever show us would be to exalt Himself as head over all, as He has done. Someone must rule creation. It is to our benefit that the most holy, righteous, loving, and powerful Being take His place as Ruler and not relegate it to a lesser being.

3. To conclude our study of the supremacy of God, we will consider a very important text from the book of Psalms. What does Psalm 113:4-6 teach us about God's absolute supremacy over all creation?

_____

_____

_____

_____

_____

NOTES: In verse 6, we read, "Who humbles Himself to behold the things that are in heaven and in the earth?" This is one of the most majestic verses in all of Scripture. It means that God is so glorious, so excellent, and so beautiful that He must condescend (*i.e.* humble Himself) to turn His eyes away from His own beauty and look at any other being or thing. All the beauty of heaven and earth combined is nothing compared to the glory of God Himself.

Chapter 36: The Titles of God's Sovereignty

In the thought and language of the Scriptures, a name can have great significance and communicate many important truths about the one who bears it. In the Scriptures are found numerous names and titles that communicate important truths about God's attributes and works. Through the study of these names, we can come to know Him in a greater and more profound way. In the following, we will consider the most important names and titles that demonstrate God's absolute sovereignty over all creation.

LORD

The English title that is most often employed in the Scriptures to communicate God's sovereignty is **Lord**. The title describes someone who has supremacy and authority over another. When applied to God, it refers to His absolute sovereignty over all creation. It is important to recognize that the title "Lord" not only communicates truth about God but also defines man's relationship to Him. If God is Lord, then man is His subject.

1. In the Scriptures, a name has great significance and communicates something about the person who bears it. What names or titles are attributed to God in the following Scriptures?

    a. L_____ of the Whole E_____ *(Psalm 97:5)*. The title "Lord" is translated from the Hebrew word **adonay**, which is the plural form of **adon**. The word denotes both lordship and ownership. In the Scriptures, the plural form is always used with reference to God to denote intensity—God is the absolute Lord of all things, without exception.

    b. L_____ of H_____ *(Daniel 5:23)*. The extension of God's lordship or sovereignty is not limited to the earth; it extends to the farthest reaches of the universe and encompasses all creation—material and spiritual.

    c. L_____ of H_____ and E_____ *(Acts 17:24)*. The title "Lord" is translated from the Greek word **kúrios**. For the Greeks, the word **kúrios** could refer to a man of high position and power or a supernatural being (*i.e.* a god). The word is used in the Septuagint (the Greek translation of the Hebrew Old Testament) in place of the Hebrew name **Yahweh** and in the New Testament to communicate the Hebrew idea of God as Lord. It is significant that the word **kúrios** is used without reservation when referencing Jesus.

    d. Lord of L_____ *(Deuteronomy 10:17; Psalm 136:3; I Timothy 6:15; Revelation 17:14; 19:16)*. In the above Old Testament texts, the title "Lord" is translated from the Hebrew word **adonay**. In the New Testament texts, the title is translated from the Greek word **kúrios**. Whatever lords there may be in the heavens or on earth, visible or invisible, whether thrones or dominions or rulers or authorities—God is Lord over all of them!

e. *Lord of K_____* *(Daniel 2:47)*. The same commentary can be made over and over again—whatever kings or lords may exist in any realm of creation, we can be assured that God rules over them with absolute and undaunted authority and power.

2. Based upon the truths communicated by the above titles (Main Point 1), write a brief explanation of the lordship of God and what it means for all men, especially for believers. Two texts that are worthy of consideration are Malachi 1:6 and Luke 6:46.

_____

_____

_____

_____

_____

_____

KING

Closely related to the title of **Lord** is that of **King**. There is probably no other title in the English language that has as much power to communicate the ideas of sovereignty, power, royalty, nobility, and majesty. In the Scriptures, God is the great King over all creation, who reigns with unsurpassed glory. His throne is in heaven, the earth is His footstool, and His kingdom endures forever.

1. In the Scriptures, a name has great significance and communicates something about the person who bears it. What names are attributed to God in the following Old Testament Scriptures?

a. *The G_____ King over all the E_____* *(Psalm 47:2, 7; Malachi 1:14)*. He is not **a** great king reigning over **a portion** of the world; rather, He is **the** great King reigning over **all** the earth without restriction of authority or limitation of jurisdiction!

b. *The King of H_____* *(Daniel 4:37)*. Even the pagan king Nebuchadnezzar recognized that the extension of God's reign is not limited to the earth but extends to the farthest reaches of the universe and encompasses all creation—material and spiritual.

c. *The G_____ King above all G_____* *(Psalm 95:1-3)*. This Scripture is not teaching that there is more than one true God. The Apostle Paul states that these so-called gods of the nations were nothing more than demons and that those who sacrificed to them sacrificed to demons (I Corinthians 10:20; see also Leviticus 17:7; Deuteronomy 32:17; Psalm 106:37). This text is simply stating that God reigns over all things—including the false idols of men and the powerful demonic influences behind them.

2. What names or titles are attributed to God in the following New Testament Scriptures?

a. *King of the N_____* (*Revelation 15:3-4*). Throughout human history, nations have arisen that have ruled over others with absolute and undisputed sovereignty (Babylon, Rome, etc.). Yet God is the King over all nations, and He rules them with absolute authority. The prophet Isaiah declared that, in comparison to God, "the nations are like a drop from a bucket and are regarded as a speck of dust on the scales" (Isaiah 40:15).

b. *The K_____ of K_____* (*I Timothy 6:15-16; Revelation 17:14; 19:16*). As Christians, we must give honor to and pray for the kings of this earth and all who are in authority (Romans 13:1; I Timothy 2:1-2). Nevertheless, there is a sense in which this world has only one true King, and to Him must our ultimate allegiance be given. The truth in this text should also lead all human authorities to humble themselves before God and submit to His will.

c. *The King E_____, I_____, I_____, the only God* (*I Timothy 1:17*). Here the divine King is described with three adjectives that demonstrate His supremacy or superiority over all other so-called kings. (1) Eternal – the word is translated from the Greek phrase **tôn aiônōn** ("of the ages"). The idea is that God is King of every age. No matter how far back through history we travel or how far forward, we will discover that God is King. (2) Immortal – the word is translated from the Greek word **áphthartos**, which also means, "imperishable, incorruptible, and undecaying." Even the greatest of all earthly kings die and turn to dust. At the moment of death, their rule comes to an end, their bodies decay, and they are weaker than an infant born into poverty. But God is immortal. There will never be a changing of the guard, He will never be voted out of office, and He will never die so that another must take His place. He will always be the King with whom we must deal. (3) Invisible – the word is translated from the Greek word **aóratos**, which denotes that God is spirit and is therefore unhindered by the physical limitations or restraints of even the most powerful rulers.

3. Based upon the truths communicated by the above titles (Main Points 1 and 2), write a brief explanation of the kingship of God and what it means for all men, especially for believers.

_____

_____

_____

_____

SOVEREIGN, RULER, AND MASTER

The three divine titles **Sovereign**, **Ruler**, and **Master** clearly communicate the absolute authority of God over His creation. The title "Sovereign" comes from the Latin prefix **super**, which means, "over" or "above." It refers to one who rules over others with authority. The title "Ruler" is derived from the Latin verb **regere**, which means, "to lead straight or guide." It refers to one who sets the standard and marks out the path with authority. The title "Master" is derived from the Latin term **magnus**, which means, "great" or "large." It refers to one who has control or mastery over something, such as a teacher who has mastered a certain area of study, an owner who has control over his property, or a ruler who reigns over his subjects. In the following Scriptures, we will learn that God is the only true Sovereign, Ruler, and Master over all creation.

1. In the Scriptures, a name has great significance and communicates something about the person who bears it. What names are attributed to God in the following Scriptures? What do they communicate to us about His sovereignty?

   a. *The B_____ and only S_____* (I Timothy 6:15-16). The word "sovereign" comes from the Greek word **dunástēs**, which denotes a ruler or potentate. It is from the same primary verb as **dúnamis**, which denotes power or might. It was often used to describe someone who ruled with a delegated authority, but this is not the case with God. He rules by His own right and power. The word "blessed" comes from the Greek word **makários**, which denotes that God exists in perfect and uninterrupted blessedness, joy, and contentment.

   b. *The R_____ over the R_____ of mankind* (Daniel 4:17). The word "ruler" comes from the Aramaic word **shallit**, which denotes one having mastery, rule, or dominance. The word "realm" is translated from the Aramaic word **malku**, which denotes a kingdom or realm. God does not just rule over individual persons or kingdoms—His rule extends over the entire realm of humanity collectively, and He is directing everything toward His desired end.

   c. *Our only M_____ and Lord* (Jude 4; see also II Timothy 2:21 and II Peter 2:1). The word "master" is translated from the Greek word **despótēs**, which denotes ownership and absolute lordship. In its oldest use, the **despótēs** was the master of the house, who ruled with absolute authority. In time, the word came to connote someone of unlimited or even tyrannical political authority—a despot. Today, this term is most often used negatively for the simple reason that absolute power corrupts fallen men absolutely.[1] However, when the term is ascribed to God in the Septuagint and the New Testament, it communicates nothing negative, for He is incorruptible. God is the rightful Owner and Lord of what He has made. His holiness and righteousness guarantee

---

[1] This is derived from the quote by English historian John Dalberg-Acton: "Power tends to corrupt, and absolute power corrupts absolutely."

that He will always use His absolute authority with perfect justice. The term ***despótēs*** is used six times in the New Testament with reference to God (Luke 2:29; Acts 4:24; II Timothy 2:21; II Peter 2:1; Jude 4; and Revelation 6:10). In II Peter 2:1 and Jude 4, the reference is specifically to Jesus Christ.

2. Based upon the truths communicated by the above titles (Main Point 1), write a brief explanation of God's sovereign mastery or rule and what it means for all men, especially for the believer.

_____

_____

_____

_____

_____

_____

_____

Chapter 37: The Extension of God's Sovereignty

It is often asked, "What are the limits of God's rule? Is there any creature or activity that is not under His government?" The Scripture's answer is clear—every living being, every created thing, and all events of history are under the sovereign government of God. He rules over all things; and nothing, including man, is beyond the boundaries of His rule. As Creator and Sustainer, He has the exclusive and unchallenged right to govern all realms and all creatures according to His will and good pleasure. He does all that He desires; there is no power in heaven, earth, or hell that can alter or hinder what He has determined.

1. The following are some of the most important declarations in the Scriptures with regard to the absolute sovereignty of God. Carefully consider each verse, and then identify the truths that are being communicated. What do they teach us about the extension of God's sovereignty?

   a. *Psalm 33:11*

   _____

   _____

   _____

   _____

   > **NOTES:** The reference to God's "heart" is an **anthropomorphic** expression [Greek: **án-thrōpos** = man + **morphê** = form]. In other words, God is simply attributing to Himself human characteristics in order to communicate a truth about Himself in a way that men can comprehend. The plans of God's heart refer to His certain and immutable decrees.

   b. *Psalm 103:19*

   _____

   _____

   _____

_____

_____

NOTES: The word "established" comes from the Hebrew verb **_kun_**, which means, "to make firm, sure, or steadfast." God's throne and His sovereign decrees are immovable and unassailable.

c. _Psalm 115:3_

_____

_____

_____

_____

NOTES: The word "pleases" comes from the Hebrew verb **_chafetz_**, which means, "to delight in or take pleasure in." Theologians commonly speak of God's good pleasure. It means that God's decisions and actions are not motivated merely by logic, calculation, or reason; and they are never driven by caprice or whim. God does that which conforms to His holiness, righteousness, and love, and that which brings Him delight.

d. _Psalm 135:6_

_____

_____

_____

_____

NOTES: The reference to heaven, earth, and the seas is a poetic way of making reference to the entirety of creation without exception. Here the psalmist goes even further by mentioning "all deeps." Every "nook and cranny" of creation, so to speak, is under God's sovereign rule.

e. *Ephesians 1:11*

_____

_____

_____

_____

_____

NOTES: The word "work" comes from the Greek word ***energéō***, which communicates not only work but also energy and efficiency. God accomplishes all things according to His will with unlimited energy and perfect efficiency.

2. The truth that God does whatever He pleases in every realm of creation is a testimony not only to His sovereignty but also to His omnipotence. He is all-powerful, and there is therefore no creature or power that can oppose Him. What do the following Scriptures teach us about this truth?

a. *II Chronicles 20:6*

_____

_____

_____

_____

b. *Job 23:13*

_____

_____

_____

_____

NOTES: The word "unique" comes from the Hebrew word ***'echad***, meaning, "one." The phrase is probably an idiom—a phrase whose meaning is determined by its usage in the common language rather than from its individual words (English example: "raining cats and dogs"). The idea communicated is that God is unchangeable or immutable (ESV/NET). The reference to "soul" is an anthropomorphic expression (*i.e.* one typically used to describe humans). For God, there is nothing impossible, unattainable, or beyond the reach of His will or desire.

c. *Proverbs 21:30-31*

_____

_____

_____

_____

3. It is important to understand that there is also a direct relationship between God's sovereignty and His ability to foresee and foretell the future. What does Isaiah 46:9-10 teach us about this truth?

_____

_____

_____

_____

NOTES: Many believers wrongly attribute God's ability to foretell the future to His omniscience, without any thought of His sovereignty. However, as this text demonstrates (v.10), God knows the future perfectly not only because He is perfectly omniscient, but also because He is absolutely sovereign. He has decreed every event from beginning to end, and He is directing all things according to what He has decreed! He knows the future not because He looks through the corridors of time and sees how all things will play out, but because He is the Author of the future and is directing all things according to His plan!

4. In Daniel 4:34-35 is found one of the greatest declarations in all the Scriptures with regard to the sovereignty of God over His creation. Summarize each of the following segments, and explain what is taught about the sovereignty of God.

a. *His dominion is an everlasting dominion. His kingdom endures from generation to generation (v.34).*

_____

_____

_____

_____

NOTES: If God's government were not everlasting, or if there were even the slightest possibility that His power could be diminished or His throne could be usurped, then it would be difficult for His people to trust in Him. The fact that God's character and sovereignty are immutable should lead us to have the greatest confidence in His promises and providence. It should lead God's enemies to raise the white flag and seek peace before it is too late.

b. *All the inhabitants of the earth are accounted as nothing (v.35).*

_____

_____

_____

_____

NOTES: We must be sure that we understand the language that is used here. It does not mean that God depreciates His creation or that He is uncaring for what He has made. One of the most astounding truths of the Scriptures is that a God so great is willing to condescend to care for us. As the psalmist inquired in amazement, "What is man that You take thought of him, and the son of man that You care for him?" The idea communicated in this text is that, in comparison to the greatness of God, all creation combined is as nothing.

c. *He does according to His will in the host of heaven and among the inhabitants of the earth (v.35).*

_____

_____

_____

_____

d. *No one can ward off His hand or say to Him, "What have you done?" (v.35).*

_____

_____

_____

_____

NOTES: The truth conveyed in this text is powerful: there is no strength in heaven or earth that can restrain God's hand, and there is no wisdom that can call Him into question or refute Him!

Chapter 38: Our Response to God as the Sovereign

God is creation's sovereign Lord and King. He rules over all creatures, actions, and things, from the greatest to the smallest. He is free to do all things according to His own will and to do them for His own glory and good pleasure. No power in heaven or on earth can hinder what He has determined. What should be man's response to such a God? The Scriptures are clear—we should render to Him **reverence** and **worship**. When the sovereignty or lordship of God is correctly understood, it moves all men to prostrate themselves before Him and to acknowledge that He alone is worthy of creation's reverence, obedience, worship, adoration, and praise.

REVERENCE AND OBEDIENCE

Man's first response to the sovereignty of God should be reverence and obedience. To revere God is to acknowledge His highest place before us as Lord and regard Him with the utmost respect and awe. Such an attitude of reverence will always result in obedience. Sovereignty implies a relationship of one exercising authority over another. If we truly acknowledge God's sovereignty, then we will place ourselves before Him in reverent submission to His will.

1. What do the following Scriptures teach us about the great and sincere reverence that is due God as the Lord and only Sovereign of creation?

   a. *Psalm 47:2*

   _____

   _____

   _____

   _____

   _____

   _____

NOTES: In this text, three titles are given to God: Lord, Most High, and great King. Any one of these by itself should be enough to fill us with the deepest reverence. How much more when all three are used together? The word "feared" comes from the Hebrew word **yare**, which in this context denotes fear, awe, and great reverence.

b. *Jeremiah 10:6-7*

_____

_____

_____

_____

_____

_____

NOTES: The call to give God the fear (Hebrew: **yare**) that is due Him is placed among three great motivations—the greatness of His might (v.6), the greatness of His sovereignty (v.7), and the greatness of His wisdom (v.7). Also notice that the passage begins with the declaration that there is none like God and ends with a repetition of the same declaration. No one is like Him; therefore, He is to be feared above all else. The question, "Who would not fear You…?" is clearly rhetorical. In light of who God is, the only logical response is to give Him the reverence that is due Him.

c. *Daniel 6:25-27*

_____

_____

_____

_____

_____

_____

NOTES: Darius was the pagan king of the Medo-Persian Empire. However, through God's deliverance of the prophet Daniel, he came to recognize that the God of Israel was the one true God. He was so impressed by God's deliverance of Daniel from the lions' den that he wrote out an official edict to all the subjects of his vast empire, demanding that all show reverence to the God of Daniel. According to his edict, men are to fear Daniel's God because: (1) He is the living God, in contrast to the lifeless idols of stone that were typically worshiped by those outside of Israel; (2) His sovereign rule is forever; and (3) He delivers, rescues, and performs signs and wonders, in contrast to the false gods of the nations, who did neither good nor bad.

2. Based upon the texts above, write your own explanation of how we should respond with reverence and awe in light of God's sovereignty.

_____

_____

_____

_____

_____

_____

_____

_____

_____

3. Having considered the reverence that is due the King of kings and Lord of lords, we will now consider the obedience that must follow all true reverence. What do the following Scriptures teach us about the obedience that is due God as the Lord and only Sovereign of creation?

a. *Psalm 66:7*

_____

_____

_____

_____

NOTES: The word "rebellious" is translated from the Hebrew verb **sarar**, which means, "to be rebellious, stubborn, obstinate, or contrary."

b. *Deuteronomy 27:10*

_____

_____

_____

_____

NOTES: In Hebrew, the phrase, "obey the Lord," is literally, "hear the voice of the Lord." The word "hear" is translated from the Hebrew word **shama**, which denotes more than simply hearing; it also includes listening to or obeying what one has heard. We hear the voice of the Lord through His Word and the specific commands that it communicates to us.

c. *Acts 5:29*

_____

_____

_____

_____

NOTES: Peter and the other apostles had been commanded by the Jewish Council to no longer teach the people in Christ's name. Their response was that they must obey God. Believers are to give honor to earthly authorities and to obey their commands whenever possible (Romans 13:1-7). However, when the commands of men contradict those of God, the believer must submit to God.

d. *James 1:22*

_____

_____

_____

_____

NOTES: The word "delude" comes from the Greek word *paralogízomai* [*pará* = beside, contrary to + *logízomai* = to reckon], which means, "to reckon wrongly, to miscalculate, to reason falsely, or to delude."

4. In Scripture and in our own day, we see the danger of confessing God to be Lord while living in a manner that contradicts our confession. How does God respond to any empty confession of His lordship?

a. *Malachi 1:6*

_____

_____

_____

_____

b. *Luke 6:46*

_____

_____

_____

_____

c. *Matthew 7:21*

_____

_____

_____

_____

NOTES: This does not mean that salvation is by works. The truth communicated is that those who have believed unto salvation will obey the Father's will. Faith will not result in a perfect life on this earth, but it will result in a life that is being changed by the power of God. In other words, faith will result in works; works are therefore the proof of faith (James 2:14-26).

WORSHIP, ADORATION, AND PRAISE

If men think it proper to give homage and honor to the kings and rulers of the earth, whose lives are mortal and whose kingdoms are frail and temporary, how much more should mankind honor the eternal King, whose kingdom endures forever! Although there are many kings and lords, God alone bears the title of **King of kings and Lord of lords**. He alone is supreme over all creation, ruling with absolute and unhindered sovereignty. The inhabitants of the earth are like grasshoppers before Him. The nations are like a drop from a bucket and regarded as a speck of dust on the scales. He reduces rulers to nothing and makes void the decisions of the most powerful among angels and men. There is no wisdom, no understanding, and no counsel against Him. He does all things according to the counsel of His own perfect will, and no creature in heaven or on earth can restrain His hand or say to Him, "What have You done?" He should therefore be the focus of all worship, adoration, and praise.

In Psalm 99:1-5 is found one of the most majestic declarations in the Old Testament about the worship that is due God as Lord and King. Read the text until you are familiar with its contents, and then answer the following questions.

1. How is God described in the following verses? What does this description of God communicate to us about His sovereign rule over creation? Complete the following declarations.

   a. *He R_____ (v.1).* From the Hebrew word **malak**, which means, "to be a king or to reign as a king." He is the great King over all the earth (Psalm 47:2, 7; Malachi 1:14), the King of heaven (Daniel 4:37), the great King above all gods (Psalm 95:1-3), and the King of kings (I Timothy 6:15-16; Revelation 17:14; 19:16).

   b. *He is E_____ above the C_____ (v.1).* We know very little about these angelic creatures. It is possible that, like the seraphim (Isaiah 6:2-3), they are among the greatest of all created beings. Yet God is enthroned above them as their Creator, Sustainer, and Lord.

   c. *He is G_____ (v.2).* From the Hebrew word **gadol**. The word is a relative term. Some men may consider themselves great in comparison to others, but God is infinitely greater than all of creation combined.

   d. *He is E_____ above all the peoples (v.2).* From the Hebrew word **rum**, which may be translated, "high, exalted, or set apart." To give us a perspective of how exalted the Lord truly is, the prophet Isaiah tells us that the earth is His footstool (Isaiah 66:1).

   e. *His name is G_____ and A_____ (v.3).* The word "awesome" is derived from the Hebrew word **yare**, which means, "to fear or revere." God is not to be feared because of some inconsistency in His nature or unrighteousness in His work, but because of His greatness and holiness.

   f. *He is H_____ (v.3).* From the Hebrew word **qadosh**, which means, "separated, marked off, placed apart, or withdrawn from common use." With regard to God, the word has at least two important meanings: (1) God is transcendent above His creation, and (2) He is transcendent above His creation's corruption.

2. How is God's reign described in verse four? What are the characteristics of His sovereign rule over creation? How should these truths impact our lives?

_____

_____

_____

_____

_____

NOTES: God's reign is marked by His strength, His love for justice, and His equity and righteousness in judgment. This should instill in believers the greatest confidence and security, and it should lead the rebellious to repent of their ways and seek reconciliation with God.

3. According to the following verses from Psalm 99:1-5, how should men respond to what God has revealed about Himself and His sovereign rule over His creation?

a. *Verse 1*

_____

_____

_____

_____

NOTES: It is important to emphasize that the trembling is not because of some inconsistency in God that would make Him capricious or untrustworthy. Rather, our trembling ought to be a response of wonder at His infinite greatness and majesty! Notice that it is not only men who should tremble—the very world itself should shake!

b. *Verse 3*

_____

_____

_____

_____

NOTES: The word "praise" comes from the Hebrew word **yadah**, which literally means, "to throw or cast." Figuratively, it means to confess or praise. In one sense, praise is simply confessing as true what God has revealed to us about Himself.

c. *Verse 5*

_____

_____

_____

_____

NOTES: The word "exalt" comes from the Hebrew word **rum**, which may also be translated, "to be high" or "to be set apart." We learned from verse two that God is exalted above the peoples; how then can we further exalt Him? To exalt God means to recognize and confess His exalted status over all creation.

Chapter 39: God Is the Lawgiver

Having considered God as Lord, we will now consider His place over creation as Lawgiver and Judge. The Scriptures teach us that God is a holy, righteous, and loving Sovereign who cares for the well-being of His creation. It is right that such a Sovereign should rule over His creation and administer justice, rewarding the good that is done and punishing the evil. According to the Scriptures, God has revealed His will to all men and will judge all men according to the standard that has been revealed to them. All creatures can be assured that God will judge them according to the strictest standards of justice and fairness. It must always be recognized that God's judgment of man is not unwarranted or cruel; rather, it is an inevitable consequence of His holy and righteous character and a necessary part of His government. A God who would forego judging wickedness would not be good or righteous. A creation where wickedness was not restrained and judged would soon self-destruct.

GOD THE LAWGIVER

The Scriptures teach us that the Creator and sovereign Lord of the universe is also its supreme Lawgiver and Judge. God has established the moral laws by which all men must live, and He holds them accountable for their obedience and disobedience. According to the Scriptures, man was not created to be **autonomous** [Greek: **autós** = self + **nómos** = law] or self-governed, but **theonomous** [Greek: **theós** = God + **nómos** = law]—under God's law.

As Lawgiver and Judge, God is both holy and righteous. The **holiness** of God refers to His separation from all that is common, profane, or sinful. The **righteousness** of God refers to the rightness and fairness of all His works and judgments. These attributes guarantee that God's law will always be appropriate or right and that His judgments will always be perfect. He will always do the right thing. On the day of His judgment, all men can be assured that God will judge them with perfect justice. Even the condemned will bow their heads and declare that the Judge of all the earth has judged them righteously.

1. In Isaiah 33:22, three very important offices are ascribed to God. Each one communicates to us something about the person and work of God and about our relationship to Him. Identify these three offices, and write a brief explanation of the truth they communicate.

    a. J_____.

    _____

    _____

    _____

    _____

NOTES: From the Hebrew word **shafat**, which refers to a judge or governor—one who decides or hands down a judgment. The Scriptures teach that God will decide the eternal fate of every member of the human race.

b. L_____.

_____

_____

_____

_____

NOTES: From the Hebrew word **chaqaq**, which literally means, "to cut in, carve, engrave, or inscribe." Figuratively, it means to decree, enact, or command something. God carved His law onto stone (Exodus 31:18) and onto the human heart (Romans 2:14-15). Heaven and earth will pass away before even the smallest letter of God's law will pass (Matthew 5:18), and it is by His law that all men will be judged.

c. K_____.

_____

_____

_____

_____

NOTES: From the Hebrew word **melek**, which denotes a king or ruler. God rules His kingdom according to His law, and He will judge the inhabitants of His kingdom (i.e. every man) according to His law. God is King, Lawgiver, and Judge. All men have rebelled against the King, have broken His law, and stand condemned before His judgment seat. In order to be saved, we need a Priest to offer a sacrifice in our place, a Prophet to lead us out of our error into truth, and a King to pardon our offenses. All these offices are found in Christ alone—He is our Priest, Prophet, and King.

2. In James 4:12 is found an extremely important truth about God. What does this Scripture teach us about God and about our relationship to Him?

_____

_____

_____

_____

NOTES: This text not only affirms that God is both Lawgiver and Judge, but it also communicates the seriousness of the matter. The final judgment will determine the eternal destiny of all men. It is not to be taken lightly. On that final day, there will only be two possible verdicts: (1) eternal salvation in heaven or (2) eternal death and destruction in hell. If we take the laws and judgments of men with a high degree of seriousness, how much more should we be concerned for the law and judgments of God! Jesus gave us the following warning: "Do not fear those who kill the body but are unable to kill the soul; but rather fear Him who is able to destroy both soul and body in hell" (Matthew 10:28).

THE FOUNDATION OF GOD'S LAW

Why has God declared some things to be "right" and others to be "wrong"? Is God's law nothing more than an arbitrary set of rules? Is there a reason behind all these commands and prohibitions? What is the true essence or heart of the law? These are very important questions. If we are to have a correct understanding of God's law, we must give them careful consideration. The following statements are helpful.

1. **God is the self-existent Creator, Sustainer, and Lord of all.** It is right for God to rule over and judge all that He has made and sustains. It is right for Him to establish His laws and hold His creatures accountable to them.

2. **God is the only basis for morality.** Why are some things "good" and other things "evil"? What is the basis for determining whether something is "right" or "wrong"? The Bible teaches that God is good. That which is like God (*i.e.* conforms to His character) is "good," and that which is not like God (*i.e.* contradicts or opposes His character) is "evil." Apart from God, there can be no laws, no right or wrong, and no standard of good or evil.

3. **God's laws are an expression of who He is.** God's laws are not arbitrary rules that He has capriciously chosen; they are a reflection of His character—His holiness, righteousness, benevolence, and so on. Sometimes, even Christians speak of the "law" as if it were some set of eternal and universal principles, independent of God and to which even God Himself is subject. However, this could not be further from the truth! It is God who established all laws, and the laws He has established are expressions of His very nature.

4. **The essence of God's law is to love Him supremely and to love others as ourselves.** This is clearly taught by Jesus to be the heart and ultimate end to which all divine law is directed (Mark 12:29-31). The knowledge that we should love God supremely and others as ourselves is written on the heart of every man, and its full implications (*i.e.* what such love involves) are spelled out in clear and specific terms in the Scriptures (*e.g.* not worshiping idols, not stealing, not murdering, etc.).

THE LAW REVEALED IN THE SCRIPTURES

The law of God is made known to men through the Scriptures. In the pages of the Bible, we learn that men ought to love God supremely and love their fellow man as themselves. It is also through the Bible that the full implications of such love are spelled out in clear and specific terms: we love God by not worshiping idols, not stealing, not murdering, and so on (Exodus 20:1-17). This written revelation of the law is unfolded with greater and greater clarity throughout the Bible, beginning in the book of Genesis and reaching its culmination in the New Testament. From Genesis to Revelation, God's will is both revealed and illustrated. For this reason, the Apostle Paul wrote in II Timothy 3:16:

> *"All Scripture is inspired by God and profitable for teaching, for reproof, for correction, for training in righteousness."*

Although God's revelation of His law in the Scriptures includes every portion of the Bible, God's will for human conduct was made known with special power and clarity on two occasions in Biblical history: (1) at the giving of the Old Covenant to Israel through Moses on Mt. Sinai (Exodus 20:1-18), and (2) at the coming of the Lord Jesus Christ—God's ultimate and final word to mankind (Hebrews 1:1-2).

THE LAW REVEALED IN THE HEART

We have learned that God is the great Lawgiver who will judge every man according to His law, but this truth brings to mind a very important and troubling question: "How can God judge every man according to His law when a great multitude of humanity has never had the privilege of knowing the Scriptures that contain this law?"

According to the Scriptures, God has revealed His unchanging moral standard to mankind in two distinct ways: (1) He has revealed His will in great detail to **some men** through the written commands of Scripture, and (2) He has revealed His will to **all men** in a general way through the law that He has written on their hearts. In both cases, the revelation of God's law is sufficient so that all men without exception will be without excuse on the Day of Judgment. Those who have had the privilege of possessing the Scriptures will be judged according to the Scriptures, and those who have only had the influence of the law written upon their hearts will be judged according to that revelation of the law. Each man will be judged according to the light he has received. As the Scriptures declare in Luke 12:47-48:

> *"And that slave who knew his master's will and did not get ready or act in accord with his will, will receive many lashes, but the one who did not know it, and committed deeds worthy of a flogging, will receive but*

*few. From everyone who has been given much, much will be required;
and to whom they entrusted much, of him they will ask all the more."*

1. As noted above, because God is the supreme Lawgiver who will judge all men according to His law, we are forced to deal with a difficult question: "How can God judge every man according to His law when a great multitude of humanity has never had the privilege of knowing the Scriptures that contain this law?" In Romans 2:12, the answer to this problem is set before us with great clarity.

   a. *According to Romans 2:12, all mankind can be divided into two distinct groups. What are these two groups?*

      (1) Those who have sinned W_____ the Law. This refers specifically to the Gentiles or pagans outside of Israel who had no knowledge of the Old Covenant Law of God as revealed in the Pentateuch (*i.e.* the first five books of the Bible) through Moses. In the wider context, it refers to all those throughout history who have lived and died without the privilege of knowing the details of the law of God revealed through the written commands of the Scriptures.

      (2) Those who have sinned U_____ the Law. This refers specifically to the nation of Israel, who had been entrusted with the Old Testament Law of God revealed through Moses. In the wider context, it refers to all those throughout history who have been privileged to know the law of God as it is revealed in detail through the written commands of the Scriptures.

   b. *According to Romans 2:12, what are the consequences of sin for both groups—those who have known the law as it is revealed in the Scriptures and those who were never privileged with such knowledge?*

   _____

   _____

   _____

   _____

   NOTES: Both groups will be judged by the law that they have received, whether it only be the law of God written on the heart or that in addition to the law of God revealed through the Scriptures.

2. It is understandable how God can rightly condemn those who have known the written code of His law and still rebelled against it, but how can He justly condemn those who have lived and died without ever having access to the Scriptures? In the following texts, two reasons are set forth that prove that God is right in judging all men, even those without the Scriptures.

a. **GOD HAS MADE HIMSELF EVIDENT TO ALL MEN THROUGH CREATION.** What does Romans 1:19-20 teach us about this truth?

_____

_____

_____

_____

_____

NOTES: This does not mean that all men know everything that may be known about God or that all men are granted the same degree of revelation. It means that all men—in every place and at all times—possess sufficient knowledge of the true and living God to be without excuse for their sins on the Day of Judgment. Although limited, God's revelation of Himself to all men has not been ambiguous or unclear. He has made it "evident" to all men that there is one true God and that He alone should be worshiped. The phrase "within them" suggests that the knowledge of the living God is not demonstrated through the works of creation alone, but that God Himself has imprinted this knowledge upon the very heart of every man. The universe that God has made proves His existence and simply acts as a confirmation of what all men already know—there is one true God, and He is worthy of worship and obedience.

b. **GOD HAS PLACED HIS LAW IN THE HEARTS OF ALL MEN.** What does Romans 2:14-15 teach us about this truth?

_____

_____

_____

_____

_____

NOTES: This does not mean that there were those among the Gentiles who obeyed God's law perfectly so as to be righteous before Him (see Romans 3:9-12). It means that even in pagan cultures there were morals and standards that agreed with God's law (*e.g.* high regard for telling the truth, duty to honor one's parents, prohibitions against murder, etc.). This stands as undeniable proof that God has written (*i.e.* imprinted or engraved) the essence of His law (love to God and love to one's fellowmen) on the heart of every man. Though multitudes are without the written code of the law revealed through the Scriptures, God has written His law on their very hearts and minds. This law is sufficient to guide men in the right way, despite not being as specific as the written law of Scripture. Therefore, all men will be held accountable on the Day of Judgment. In verse 15, Paul mentions the conscience, which refers to a moral sense of right and wrong within every man, which defends him when he obeys God's law and accuses him in every act of disobedience to God. It is possible for the conscience to be rejected (I Timothy 1:19) to the point that it no longer functions as a moral compass. Paul refers to this frightful state as being turned over to the "degrading passions" of one's own corrupt heart (Romans 1:24, 26) or having the conscience seared as with a hot iron (I Timothy 4:2).

Chapter 40: God Is the Judge

According to the Scriptures, God has revealed His will to all men and will judge all men according to the standard that has been revealed to them. All creatures can be assured that God will judge them according to the strictest standards of justice and fairness. It must always be recognized that God's judgment of man is not unwarranted or cruel, but an inevitable consequence of His holy and righteous character and a necessary part of His government. A God who would forego judging wickedness would not be good or righteous. A creation where wickedness was not restrained and judged would soon self-destruct.

THE OMNISCIENT OBSERVER

In previous chapters, we learned that God is both holy and righteous and that these attributes stand as an eternal and immutable guarantee that His judgments will always be in accordance with the strictest rules of equity and justice. Before we consider the Bible's teaching regarding the judgment of God, we must review another divine attribute that is equally essential if His judgments are to be infallible—the omniscience of God. The word "omniscience" comes from the Latin word **omnisciens** [**omnis** = all + **sciens**, from **scire** = to know] and denotes the attribute of possessing all knowledge. The omniscience of God means that He possesses perfect knowledge of everything, without having to search out or discover the facts. He knows all things past, present, and future—immediately, effortlessly, simultaneously, and exhaustively. There is nothing hidden from God; every creature, deed, and thought is before Him like an open book. God not only knows all the facts, but He also interprets them with perfect wisdom and absolute fidelity. There is never the slightest difference between God's knowledge and reality. The omniscience of God not only proves that He is worthy to judge His creation, but it also guarantees that His judgments will always be perfect. God will always judge according to His perfect knowledge of all the facts.

1. In the following Scriptures, three words are used to describe God's omniscience. Through our understanding of these words, we can begin to grasp something of the greatness of His knowledge. Identify each word according to the verse given.

   a. *God's knowledge is P_____ (Job 37:16).* Translated from the Hebrew word **tamim**, which denotes that which is whole, complete, entire, blameless, and lacking in nothing.

   b. *God's understanding is I_____ (Psalm 147:4-5).* Translated from the Hebrew word **ayin**, which denotes that which is innumerable or beyond counting. Other synonyms include "endless," "inscrutable," "unfathomable," and "unsearchable."

   c. *God's understanding is I_____ (Isaiah 40:28).* Translated from the Hebrew word **ayin** (see definition above).

2. The Scriptures affirm that nothing exists outside of the reach of God's knowledge. He knows all things past, present, and future—immediately, effortlessly, simultaneously, and exhaustive-

ly. Such knowledge not only proves that He is worthy to judge His creation, but it also guarantees that His judgments will always be perfect. God will always judge according to His perfect knowledge of all the facts. What do the following Scriptures teach us about this truth?

a. *Job 34:21-23*

_____

_____

_____

_____

b. *Proverbs 5:21; 15:3*

_____

_____

_____

_____

c. *Proverbs 15:11; Jeremiah 17:10*

_____

_____

_____

_____

d. *Hebrews 4:13*

_____

_____

_____

_____

3. According to the Scriptures, there is no depth or secret in the heart of man that is beyond the reach of God's knowledge. What do the following Scriptures teach us about this truth?

   a. *God alone knows the H_____ of all men (I Kings 8:39).*

   b. *God T_____ the H_____ and M_____ (Psalm 7:9).*

   c. *God knows the T_____ of man (Psalm 94:11).*

   d. *God will J_____ the S_____ of all men (Romans 2:16).*

4. In light of the Scriptures we have studied, explain how the omniscience of God not only proves that He is worthy to judge His creation, but also acts as a guarantee that His judgment will always be perfect.

   _____

   _____

   _____

   _____

   _____

   _____

THE DIVINE JUDGE

Having reviewed the omniscience of God, we will now consider His place as Judge of all. The Scriptures teach us that God is a holy, righteous, and loving Sovereign who cares for the well-being of His creation. Such a Sovereign must administer justice, rewarding the good and punishing the evil. Because of God's holiness, righteousness, and omniscience, all creatures can be assured that He will judge them according to the strictest standards of justice and fairness. Again, it must always be recognized that God's judgment of man is not unwarranted or cruel, but an inevitable consequence of His holy and righteous character and a necessary part of His government. A God who would forego judging wickedness would not be good or righteous. A creation where wickedness was not restrained and judged would soon self-destruct.

1. In the Scriptures, a name has great significance and communicates something about the person who bears it. What are the names given to God in the following Scriptures?

   a. *The J_____ of all the E_____ (Genesis 18:25).* The word "judge" is translated from the Hebrew word ***shaphat***, which means, "to judge, govern, or render a decision." It is important to note that God does not have a limited jurisdiction; He will give the final verdict for every human being upon the earth.

b. *The J_____ of A_____* (Hebrews 12:23). The word "judge" is translated from the Greek word **kritês**, which comes from the verb **krínō**, which means, "to judge or decide." Again, the emphasis is that God's jurisdiction has no spatial or temporal limitations. He will judge all creatures in the heavens and on the earth. There is no place or creature beyond His jurisdiction and no statute of limitations.

2. The above titles reveal God to be Judge of all. Now we will consider two titles that reveal something of His integrity.

   a. *What are the names given to God in the following Scriptures?*

   (1) The R_____ Judge (Psalm 7:11; II Timothy 4:8). In Psalm 7:11, this word comes from the Hebrew word **tsaddiq**, which denotes righteousness or blamelessness. In II Timothy 4:8, it comes from the Greek word **díkaios**, which denotes righteousness, correctness, and innocence. On the Day of Judgment, God will be blameless in all His judgments. As Moses declared, "The Rock! His work is perfect, for all His ways are just; a God of faithfulness and without injustice, righteous and upright is He" (Deuteronomy 32:4).

   (2) A God of J_____ (Isaiah 30:18). From the Hebrew word **mishpat**, which denotes justice, as coming from a judge, lawgiver, or king. God's rule is just, His laws are just, and His judgments are just. Justice marks all aspects of God's government.

   b. *What do the above names reveal to us about the righteousness of God's character and the rightness of His judgments? Write your thoughts.*

   _____

   _____

   _____

   _____

   _____

3. From the names of God, we have learned that He is a just and righteous Judge. In the following, we will consider some of the key passages in Scripture that affirm the rightness and fairness of God's judgments. Summarize in your own words the truths conveyed in each text.

   a. *Genesis 18:25*

   _____

   _____

_____

_____

NOTES: Abraham's question is rhetorical, and awaits an affirmative answer. Throughout the ages, God has proven that He is a just God, whose works and judgments are blameless. To be contrary to God's determination or to be opposed to His judgment is to be wrong.

b. *Psalm 96:10-13*

_____

_____

_____

_____

NOTES: Three key words are used in this text to communicate the integrity of God's judgment: (1) equity – from the Hebrew word **meshar**, which denotes evenness, fairness, and uprightness; (2) righteousness – from the Hebrew word **tzedeq**, which denotes rightness, accuracy, and fairness; and (3) faithfulness – from the Hebrew word **emunah**, which denotes steadfastness, honesty, and fidelity.

c. *Isaiah 5:16*

_____

_____

_____

_____

NOTES: The primary truth communicated in this text is that the Lord will be vindicated, proven right, and shown to be holy when He judges. At the Final Judgment, there will be no doubt as to God's righteous and holy character or the equity of His judgments. The New English Translation reads, "The LORD who commands armies will be exalted when he punishes, the sovereign God's authority will be recognized when he judges."

Chapter 41: The Certainty of Judgment

Contemporary culture demonstrates little concern for divine judgment. We live in an age of moral relativism in which any mention of a just God is ridiculed as primitive. The slightest suggestion that mankind and human history are heading toward a Final Judgment is met with either anger or mockery. This is an age like that described by the Apostle Peter when he wrote:

> "Know this first of all, that in the last days mockers will come with their mocking, following after their own lusts, and saying, 'Where is the promise of His coming? For ever since the fathers fell asleep, all continues just as it was from the beginning of creation.'" (II Peter 3:3-4)

Regardless of the whims and railings of contemporary man, the testimony of Scripture is sure—there is a Day of Final Judgment coming upon the world. It will be a day in which God and His righteousness will be vindicated and every man will be rewarded according to what he has done.

THE CERTAINTY OF JUDGMENT

1. In the book of Psalms are found two passages of Scripture that beautifully and powerfully set forth the certainty of the Day of Judgment. Summarize the truths communicated in each text.

   a. *Psalm 9:7-8*

   _____

   _____

   _____

   _____

   > **NOTES:** The word "abide" is translated from the Hebrew word **yashav**, which means, "to sit." Based on the context (v.4), the idea is that God sits enthroned. The word "established" is translated from the Hebrew word **kun**, which means, "to prepare, fix, or make firm." The eternal God, who does not change and who rules forever, has prepared His throne for judgment. It **will** come to pass.

   b. *Psalm 96:10-13*

   _____

   _____

NOTES: The future and final judgment of the world is an established fact of Scripture. For the righteous, it will be a day of rejoicing, as creation is finally liberated from the curse and power of sin (Romans 8:19-22). But for the wicked, it will be a day of condemnation.

2. In the book of Ecclesiastes, we find still more testimony to the certainty of judgment. Summarize the truths communicated by each of the following texts.

   a. *Ecclesiastes 3:16-17*

_____

_____

_____

_____

NOTES: The entire course of human history is marked by injustice of every kind—the wicked often prosper, and the just are often condemned. The injustice of this present age has caused many to doubt that God is just or that there will be a final day of reckoning when all wrongs will be righted. Nevertheless, the Scriptures affirm that God will judge both the righteous and the wicked!

   b. *Ecclesiastes 11:9*

_____

_____

_____

_____

NOTES: The main idea is that every action on this earth will have eternal consequences. All men, especially the youth, for whom death and judgment seem so remote, must live in light of this truth.

c. *Ecclesiastes 12:14*

_____

_____

_____

_____

3. The certainty of final judgment is not only an Old Testament doctrine, but it is also set forth in the New Testament with great clarity. What do the following texts from the New Testament teach us about this truth?

a. *Acts 17:31-32*

_____

_____

_____

_____

NOTES: The word "fixed" comes from the Greek word ***hístēmi***, which means, "to stand, set in place, appoint, establish, or confirm." The truth communicated is clear—the Day of Judgment has been fixed by the immutable decree of God.

b. *Hebrews 9:27*

_____

_____

_____

_____

NOTES: The word "appointed" comes from the Greek word ***apókeimai***, which means, "to be laid away," "to be laid up in store," or "to be reserved." Judgment is as certain as death.

c. *Revelation 22:12*

_____

_____

_____

_____

NOTES: The word "quickly" comes from the Greek word **tachú**, which may also be translated, "swiftly" or "promptly." It is important to realize that the idea is not that Jesus would come in a few years or decades, but that His return would always be imminent and that each generation should therefore prepare for it. Some dismiss this prophecy on the grounds that nearly two thousand years have passed and still there is no sign of His coming. But this mockery of the Word of God is exactly what Peter predicted: "Know this first of all, that in the last days mockers will come with their mocking, following after their own lusts, and saying, 'Where is the promise of His coming? For ever since the fathers fell asleep, all continues just as it was from the beginning of creation'" (II Peter 3:3-4).

THE FINAL JUDGMENT

We will conclude our study of the judgment of God with one of the most awesome passages in all the Scriptures regarding the Final Judgment. Read Revelation 20:11-13 several times until you are familiar with its contents, and then answer the following questions.

1. How is the judgment throne of God described in verse 11? What truths does this description communicate to us?

_____

_____

_____

_____

NOTES: The throne is described as great and white. The first adjective "great" is translated from the Greek word **mégas**. The combined magnitude and glory of all the thrones of men since the dawn of time would be miniscule in comparison to the throne of God. The second adjective "white" denotes the holiness and purity not only of the throne but also of the One seated upon it.

2. According to verse 11, where is God seated? What truths does this communicate to us about God and His relationship to His creatures?

_____

_____

_____

_____

_____

NOTES: The fact that God is sitting upon the throne communicates that His sovereignty is absolute and undisputed. He governs the world effortlessly and without the least concern of being overthrown. He directs the most momentous and decisive events in the history of the universe without the slightest difficulty or strain.

3. In verse 11, it is written that heaven and earth will flee away from God and that no place will be found for them. What are the main truths being communicated?

_____

_____

_____

_____

NOTES: The two main truths communicated are: (1) the awesome presence of God manifested in judgment and (2) the passing away of the former heaven and earth in order to make way for the new.

4. According to verse 12, who will be standing before the judgment throne of God on the Great Day of Judgment? According to verse 13, will any be able to escape or hide on that day?

_____

_____

_____

_____

NOTES: The word "Hades" in verse 13 is most likely a reference to the grave or the abode of the dead. Men will find no hiding place in the deepest sea, the darkest tomb, or the lowest regions of hell. All will be called up to stand before God on the awesome day of His judgment.

5. According to verses 12-13, what do the "books" represent? What is the basis upon which God will judge every man?

_____

_____

_____

_____

NOTES: All men will be judged according to their deeds as they have been recorded before the throne of God. The only ones who will be saved on that day are those whose names have been written in the book of life—those who have trusted in Christ and His perfect work of salvation on their behalf (v.15).

6. How should all men live in light of the certainty of future and final judgment? Summarize your thoughts below.

_____

_____

_____

_____

_____

_____

Chapter 42: God Is the Savior

We will conclude this study of the doctrine of God with an extensive look at the good news that the King, Lawgiver, and Judge of the universe is also the Savior. In this chapter, we will consider the God who saves and His plan for our salvation. In the chapters that follow, we will specifically consider the roles of the Father, the Son, and the Holy Spirit in our salvation. We will learn that our salvation is the work of the entire Trinity—Father, Son, and Spirit.

THE GOD WHO SAVES

In this section, we will look at the texts of Scripture that affirm the saving work of God on behalf of sinful men. Not only will we learn that God is willing to save, but we will also discover that He alone has the power to save.

1. What are the names that are ascribed to God in the following texts from both the Old and New Testaments? What do they affirm about God?

   a. S_____ *(Psalm 17:7). From the Hebrew word* **yasha**, *which may also be translated, "deliverer." Notice that God is Savior of those who seek refuge in Him.*

   b. S_____ *and* R_____ *(Isaiah 60:16). The word "Savior" comes from the Hebrew word* **yasha** *(see definition above). The word "Redeemer" is translated from the Hebrew verb* **ga'al**, *which means, "to buy back or act as a kinsman," as set forth in Leviticus 25:25 and illustrated in the life of Boaz (Ruth 4:1-15).*

   c. *God our* S_____ *(Titus 3:4; I Timothy 2:3). From the Greek word* **sōtêr**, *which may also be translated, "deliverer," "rescuer," or "preserver."*

2. How is God described in the following texts? What do these descriptions teach us about His saving work?

   a. *Psalm 3:8; 37:39*

   _____

   _____

   _____

NOTES: The idea is that salvation comes from God. It is His prerogative. He alone is able to save or deliver. The reference to the righteous does not point to people whose lives are marked by moral perfection, but to those who are trusting and relying upon God and His salvation. The righteous shall live by faith (Habakkuk 2:4).

b. *Psalm 68:19-20*

_____

_____

_____

c. *Psalm 74:12*

_____

_____

_____

NOTES: The word "deliverance" comes from the Hebrew word **yeshuah**, which may also be translated, "salvation."

d. *Jonah 2:9*

_____

_____

_____

NOTES: Because of Jonah's rebellion against God's call, he was languishing in the belly of a great fish at the bottom of the sea. His salvation was a human impossibility. God alone could save him. The same may be said of every man.

3. The Scriptures teach us not only that God is Savior but also that He is the **only** Savior. What do Isaiah 43:11 and Isaiah 45:21 teach us about this truth?

_____

_____

_____

_____

NOTES: These texts are extremely important for two reasons: (1) they demonstrate that salvation is exclusively the work of God, and thereby (2) they prove the deity of Jesus Christ. In the New Testament, Christ is called "Savior," and even "the Savior of the world" (John 4:42). If Christ is not God in the fullest sense of the term, then He cannot be Savior. By extension, if Christ is Savior, then He must truly be God!

4. According to Isaiah 45:22, what is God's call to all men? How should all men respond? What part do we as Christians have in this call to the ends of earth?

_____

_____

_____

_____

5. According to I Chronicles 16:23-24 and Psalm 96:1-3, how should we as Christians respond to God's salvation?

_____

_____

_____

_____

GOD'S PLAN OF SALVATION

In the previous section, we learned that God is the God who saves. We will now learn that God's work of salvation was determined and designed before man ever fell, even before the foundation of the world!

1. I Peter 1:20 communicates to us something very important about Christ. What does this text teach us about God's plan of salvation?

_____

_____

NOTES: The word "foreknown" comes from the Greek word ***proginôskō*** [***pró*** = before + ***ginôskō*** = to know]. In the Scriptures, the word denotes more than mere knowledge—it also denotes choice. The text proves that, before the world was created, the Father had already determined or decreed to send His Son to die for the sins of His people. Furthermore, this text proves that the Father also determined the exact time that He would send Christ. In Galatians 4:4, Paul confirms this truth: "But when the fullness of time came, God sent forth His Son."

2. In Ephesians 1, we find further proof that God's plan of salvation reaches back before the creation of the world. Read Ephesians 1:3-6 until you are familiar with its contents, and then complete the following exercises.

   a. *What does Ephesians 1:4 teach us about God's plan of salvation?*

      (1) When did God choose His people?

NOTES: The word "chose" comes from the Greek word ***eklégō***, which means, "to select, elect, or pick out." The word is often used in the Septuagint (the Greek translation of the Old Testament) with regard to God's unmerited choice of the nation of Israel (Deuteronomy 7:7-8). The phrase, "before the foundation of the world," refers to the eternal counsels of God before the world was made.

      (2) In whom did God choose His people? What does this mean?

NOTES: How could God choose a people like us, who were morally corrupt and guilty of innumerable sins? He chose us in the Son and in light of His work on Calvary! Before the foundation of the world, God both chose His people and determined the way in which He would reconcile them to Himself.

(3) For what purpose did God choose His people?

_____

_____

_____

_____

NOTES: God's election of His people in Christ before the foundation of the world has a moral aim or goal—that we would be holy and blameless before Him. We are already these things now "in Christ"—that is, **positionally**. However, it is also God's desire that we become holy and blameless in our daily lives—that is, **practically**.

b. *What does Ephesians 1:5 teach us about God's plan of salvation?*

(1) To what did God predestine every believer?

_____

_____

_____

NOTES: The word "predestined" comes from the Greek word **proorízō** [**pró** = before + **horízō** = to mark off by boundaries, to determine], which means, "to predetermine or foreordain." Before the foundation of the world, God predetermined that His chosen people would be adopted as His sons and daughters and be His heirs (Romans 8:17; Galatians 4:7; Ephesians 3:6).

(2) Through whom have we received adoption? What does this mean?

_____

_____

_____

_____

NOTES: Our adoption is not through our merit or worth, but through the person and work of Christ on our behalf. This truth both humbles us and instills confidence within us. Our position before God is not founded upon our feeble efforts, but upon Christ's perfect and immutable work on our behalf.

(3) What was God's motivation for adopting us?

_____

_____

_____

_____

NOTES: The phrase "kind intention" is translated from the single Greek word **eu-dokía**, which literally means, "good pleasure." "Kind intention of His will" can also be translated, "purpose of His will" (ESV) or "pleasure of His will" (NET). God loved us because He is love (I John 4:8) and because He determined to set His love upon us (Deuteronomy 7:7-8). God adopted us because it pleased Him to do so!

c. _According to Ephesians 1:6, why did God design and decree our salvation? What was the great and final end?_

_____

_____

_____

_____

NOTES: The ultimate purpose for which God saved us is His own glory. His work of salvation is a demonstration of His glorious grace and will result in ceaseless praise from men and angels throughout all eternity.

3. In Romans 8:29-30, we find what is often referred to as the "Golden Chain of Salvation," because in these two verses we see God's plan of salvation from beginning to end. Read the text several times until you are familiar with its contents, and then identify each link of the chain.

a. God F_____ us (v.29). From the Greek word **proginôskō** [**pró** = before + **ginôskō** = to know]. In the Scriptures, the word denotes more than mere knowledge; it also denotes choice. The same word is used in I Peter 1:20 with regard to Christ being "foreknown before the foundation of the world." This does not mean that God in His omniscience merely foresaw that Christ would redeem His people, but that God specifically chose Christ for the task.

b. God P_____ us (vv.29-30). From the Greek word **proorízō** [**pró** = before + **horízō** = to mark off by boundaries, to determine], which means, "to predetermine or foreordain." Before the foundation of the world, God predetermined that His chosen people should become conformed to the image of His Son.

c. God C_____ us (v.30). From the Greek word **kaléō**, which means, "to call, summon, or invite." God chose us and predestined us before the foundation of the world, but He called us at a specific time in our lives through the preaching of the gospel. This truth is set forth clearly in Galatians 1:15-16. In this text, Paul declared that God had set him apart even from his mother's womb (election and predestination), but then called him through the gospel at the specific time in Paul's life when it most pleased God to do so.

d. God J_____ us (v.30). All those who have been effectively called through the preaching of the gospel and the regenerating work of the Spirit do come to faith in Christ and are justified. The word comes from the Greek word **dikaióō**, which means, "to show or declare to be righteous." In the context of our salvation, justification is a forensic or legal term. Because of the perfect work of Christ on behalf of the believer, God is able to legally declare him or her perfectly righteous before Him.

e. God G_____ us (v.30). From the Greek word **doxázō**, which means, "to think, render, or esteem glorious." The glorification of the believer refers to his final standing before God in his resurrected and perfected body; a body conformed to the image of Christ and freed forever from the power of sin. Here Paul refers to the believer's final glorification as already complete. This is probably due to Paul's great confidence in God and His sovereign decrees—the God who began a good work in the believer will perfect it (Philippians 1:6). It is important to note that there is only one stage of our salvation that Paul seems to have omitted—our sanctification (*i.e.* our progressive growth in conformity to Christ), which occurs between our justification and our final glorification. Since glorification is the aim or goal of the process of sanctification, Paul may have simply skipped over the process in order to emphasize the goal that will certainly be attained in the life of every believer by the sovereign power of God.

Chapter 43: The Father's Work of Salvation

The God who designed a plan for His people's salvation also acted (and still acts) in human history to carry out that plan. In the pages below, we will consider several great truths regarding the Father's role in the salvation of His people: God the Father sent His Son, imputed our sin to His Son, punished His Son, raised His Son from the dead, exalted His Son to His right hand, and now calls all men to repent and believe.

THE FATHER SENT HIS SON

One of the greatest mistakes made by even sincere believers is attributing the divine work of salvation to Christ alone. In some cases, Christ's work is even portrayed as saving us from the Father! However, such an idea is clearly contrary to the Scriptures. We must always remember that our salvation begins with God the Father, and it is because of His love for us that He sent His only Son.

1. For good reason, John 3:16 is one of the most beloved verses in all of Scripture. What does this text teach us about the Father and His role in our salvation?

    _____

    _____

    _____

    _____

    NOTES: The little adverb "so" comes from the Greek word *hoútōs*, which may denote either the extent to which God loved the world (*i.e.* God loved the world so much that He gave His Son) or the manner in which God loved the world (*i.e.* in this way God loved the world—that He gave His Son).

2. According to the following texts, why did God send His Son into the world? What does each text teach us about the Father and His role in our salvation?

    a. *John 3:17*

    _____

    _____

_____

_____

_____

_____

b. *I John 4:14*

_____

_____

_____

_____

_____

THE FATHER IMPUTED OUR SIN TO HIS SON

God the Father did not send His Son into this world merely to teach us truths about God or give us principles by which we might live a life that would be pleasing to Him. God sent His Son into this world to die as an atoning sacrifice in our place. For this to happen, it was necessary for God to impute our sin to His sinless Son. The word "impute" comes from the Latin verb ***imputare*** [***im*** = in, toward + ***putare*** = reckon], which means, "to reckon to one's account." On the cross, the Father reckoned our sin to His Son's account. This is one of the greatest doctrines of the Christian faith.

1. According to Romans 8:3, in what kind of body did God send His Son?

_____

_____

_____

_____

NOTES: In the incarnation, the Son of God did not take to Himself a body like that of mankind prior to the fall; rather, His body, though untainted by sin, was subject to all the terrible consequences of our fallen race. As a man, He was subject to the same limitations, frailties, afflictions, and anguishes of fallen humanity. It would have indeed been a great humiliation if the Son had taken the nature of pre-fall humanity, when it was in its full glory and strength. However, His humiliation was even greater than this, as He was sent in the "likeness of sinful flesh"!

2. According to II Corinthians 5:21, what did God the Father do to His Son while He was upon the cross? What does this teach us about the doctrine of imputation?

NOTES: God made Christ to be sin in the same way that the believer is made to be "the righteousness of God." The moment a person believes in Jesus, he is pardoned of his sin, and the righteousness of Christ is imputed to him or placed into his account. God legally declares him to be righteous and treats him as righteous. When Christ hung upon the cross, He did not become corrupt or unrighteous; rather, God imputed our sins to Him, legally declared Him to be guilty, and treated Him as guilty.

THE FATHER PUNISHED HIS SON

It was not enough for the Son to bear our sins; it was also necessary that He suffer the wrath of God and die in our place as a sin-bearing Substitute. Through the Son's suffering and death, the demands of God's justice against us were satisfied, and the wrath of God against us was appeased. Only in this way could God both maintain His justice and justify the sinner.

1. In Isaiah 53:4-5 is found one of the most important texts in all the Scriptures regarding the nature of Christ's suffering and death. What did God the Father do to His only Son as He hung on the cross of Calvary?

NOTES: Seven words are used to describe Christ's suffering under the wrath of God—He was stricken, smitten, afflicted, pierced, crushed, chastened, and scourged. The New English Translation provides helpful insight into the meaning of this text: "...we thought he was being punished, attacked by God, and afflicted for something he had done. [But] he was wounded because of our rebellious deeds, crushed because of our sins; he endured punishment that made us well; because of his wounds we have been healed."

2. In Isaiah 53:10, we find another extremely important text with regard to the nature of Christ's suffering on Calvary. How does this text affirm what we learned in Isaiah 53:4-5?

_____

_____

_____

_____

NOTES: The word "pleased" is translated from the Hebrew word ***chaphets***, which means, "to delight in, be pleased with, or desire." God did not gain some sadistic pleasure by crushing His own Son under the full weight of His wrath; rather, He was pleased that through Christ's suffering and death the will of God was accomplished and the way of salvation was opened for His people. The word "crush" comes from the Hebrew word ***daka***, which means, "to crush, smite, or break in pieces." Christ was crushed by the Father and put to grief so that His people might be saved through His suffering and death.

THE FATHER RAISED AND EXALTED HIS SON

God the Father sent His Son into the world in the likeness of sinful flesh; He imputed our sins to Him and crushed Him under the full force of His wrath. Through the death of His Son, the Father made atonement or full payment for our sin. Then, on the third day, He raised His Son from the dead, and He later exalted Him to the place of honor at His right hand as the Lord of all and the Savior of those who believe. Having proven His own authority by raising Christ from the dead and having proven Christ's authority through His exaltation, the Father now declares that all men should repent, and He commands that they believe in the name of His Son Jesus Christ.

1. THE FATHER RAISED HIS SON FROM THE DEAD. The following Scriptures testify that the resurrection of Christ was the work of God the Father. Summarize each text in your own words.

   a. *Acts 2:32; 3:15*

   _____

   _____

_____

_____

_____

b. *Romans 6:4*

_____

_____

_____

_____

NOTES: The phrase, "glory of the Father," is most likely a reference to God's glorious power (see also Ephesians 1:19-20).

2. THE FATHER EXALTED HIS SON TO HIS RIGHT HAND. Having raised His Son from the dead, the Scriptures teach that God also highly exalted Him as Lord of all and Savior of those who believe. What do the following Scriptures teach us about this truth?

a. *Philippians 2:9-11*

_____

_____

_____

_____

b. *Acts 5:30-31*

_____

_____

_____

NOTES: In this context, Peter is speaking specifically to the nation of Israel, but the truth can be applied to all peoples. God has raised and exalted His Son as the Savior of all who believe.

3. **THE FATHER NOW CALLS ALL MEN TO REPENT AND BELIEVE.** God raised His Son from the dead and exalted Him as Lord and Savior. According to the following Scriptures, how should every man respond to this great work of God? What has the Father declared and commanded?

a. *Acts 17:30-31*

_____

_____

_____

_____

_____

NOTES: The phrase, "overlooked the times of ignorance," is a reference to the long-standing ignorance and idolatry of the Gentiles. It does not mean that they were not held accountable for their sin, but only that God demonstrated patience toward them. "He permitted all the nations go their own ways" (Acts 14:16) and restrained His wrath against them with a view to Christ's coming and the offering of the gospel to all.

b. *I John 3:23*

_____

_____

_____

_____

_____

NOTES: Believing is more than just giving mental or intellectual assent. It involves trust, reliance, and dependence. To believe in Jesus is to entrust one's life and eternal well-being to the person, promises, and will of God in Christ.

245

Chapter 44: The Son's Work of Salvation

Part One: The Nature of the Son's Work

Having considered the saving work of God with special emphasis on the work of the Father, we will now consider the saving work of God the Son. As we study this subject in the next few chapters, we will see: (1) the essentiality of the Son's work; (2) the Son's willingness to fulfill the plan designed by the Father before the foundation of the world; and (3) the uniqueness of the Son's person and work—His is the only name by which we must be saved (Acts 4:12).

THE SON OUR SAVIOR

1. Identify the names that are ascribed to the Son in the following texts that clearly point to the Son as Savior.

   a. *H_____ of salvation (Luke 1:69).* From the Greek word **kéras**, which literally means, "horn." In the animal kingdom, the horn is a means of both defense and attack. Thus, it was often used figuratively in the Old Testament to denote power and strength (*e.g.* I Samuel 2:1, 10; II Samuel 22:3; Psalm 18:2; 89:17, 24; 132:17). The salvation of fallen man is beyond the power of everyone but God. Christ, as God, possesses more than the required strength to secure and to preserve our salvation.

   b. *S_____ of the world (John 4:42; I John 4:14).* From the Greek word **sōtêr**, which can also be translated, "deliverer" or "rescuer." It would be very wrong to take this title as an argument for universalism (the belief that all of humanity will be saved in the end). Rather, it teaches us that Christ's saving work is not limited to one ethnic group or geographical area; it is global in its effectiveness.

   c. *O_____ Savior (Titus 3:6).* Literally, "the savior of us." The importance of this small possessive pronoun cannot be overemphasized. At least two truths are communicated. First, the Son is the One who saves, and we are the ones who are saved. Salvation is His work, and we are the recipients of it. Secondly, He is not the Savior of all, but of those who believe. We must embrace Him and receive His salvation personally and individually. He must be **our** Savior.

   d. *D_____ (Romans 11:26).* Translated from the Greek verb **rhúomai**, which is related to the verb **erúō**, which literally means, "to drag." The idea communicated is that of dragging someone from danger and thereby rescuing or saving them. In the New Testament, the Son of God is described as the One who rescues us from the wrath to come (I Thessalonians 1:10), rescues us from our body of death (Romans 7:24-25), and rescues us from every evil deed (II Timothy 4:18). As both God and Man, the Son is uniquely qualified to deliver His people.

2. In Luke 4:14-21, Luke records the initiation of Jesus' public ministry. In verses 18-19, Jesus reads a text from the prophet Isaiah regarding the Messiah or Christ who would come (Isa-

iah 61:1-2). What does this text tell us about the saving purpose of the Son's incarnation and earthly ministry?

_____

_____

_____

_____

NOTES: The word "anointed" comes from the Greek verb **chrīō** and the Hebrew verb **mashach**, from which the title "messiah" (*i.e.* "anointed one") is derived. In the Old Testament, the priests and kings were anointed with oil as a sign of their divine appointment or commission. The Holy Spirit anointed the Son as the Messiah, who would both proclaim and accomplish the salvation of God's people.

3. According to the following texts from the Gospel of Luke, what did Jesus teach regarding His mission? Why did the Son of God take on flesh and dwell among men?

   a. *Luke 5:31-32*

_____

_____

_____

_____

NOTES: Jesus is not teaching that there are two groups of people in the world—sinners who need salvation and the righteous who need nothing. He is simply stating the purpose of His mission—the salvation of the sinners. The great problem of the Pharisees and their scribes was that they did not recognize that they were also sinners and in need of a physician.

   b. *Luke 19:10*

_____

_____

_____

_____

NOTES: To fully understand this statement it is important to consider the entire context. Jesus is being criticized for entering the house of an infamous sinner named Zaccheus.

4. In the previous two questions, we considered several texts that set forth Christ's mission to save sinners. How is this illustrated in the following parables from Luke 15? Briefly summarize the central truth that each parable teaches about Christ's purpose and willingness to save.

    a. *The Lost Sheep (Luke 15:3-7)*

    _____

    _____

    _____

    _____

    b. *The Lost Coin (Luke 15:8-10)*

    _____

    _____

    _____

    _____

    c. *The Prodigal Son (Luke 15:11-24)*

    _____

    _____

    _____

    _____

NOTES: In each of these illustrations, the emphasis is not on the worth of the one being saved, but on the love of the One who is saving. The value of one sheep is miniscule in comparison to one hundred; a lost coin is often not worth the time and energy required to find it; and the young prodigal was not deserving of the father's affections or the honor he bestowed upon him. In a similar manner, the Son was willing to make the greatest sacrifice and pay the highest price—not because of our worth or merit, but because of His great love with which He determined to love us!

5. In John 10:10-11, we find still another powerful declaration regarding the Son of God and the reason He took on flesh and dwelled among men. Summarize its important truths in your own words.

_____

_____

_____

_____

_____

_____

NOTES: The "thief" is likely a reference to the false prophets, false messiahs, and hypocritical religious leaders who appeared in Israel before the coming of the true Christ. Unlike them, Christ proved the integrity of His mission and His willingness to save by His great sacrifice on behalf of His people.

THE UNIQUENESS OF THE SON'S SAVING WORK

One of the most important and scandalous claims of the Christian faith is that Jesus is not just *a* savior, but He is *the* Savior. The Scriptures unequivocally state that outside of Christ and His redeeming work on Calvary there is no salvation. The Old Testament saints believed God, and it was credited to them as righteousness (Romans 4:3; Galatians 3:6). However, such pardon could be bestowed and such righteousness accredited only because one day Christ would come and atone for their sins. The New Testament saints (and all those after them who believe) are saved in the same manner—through the atoning death of Christ and faith in the promise that whoever believes in Him will not perish but have everlasting life (John 3:16).

1. According to the following Scriptures, what means has God appointed through which man might be saved?

a. *Acts 5:31*

_____

_____

_____

_____

_____

_____

NOTES: Repentance and faith cannot remove the guilt of sin unless the demands of God's justice against the sinner are satisfied. God can grant forgiveness of sin to those who repent and believe only because Christ has atoned for their sin on Calvary. Thus, it is only through Christ's person and work that we can be saved.

b. *I Thessalonians 5:9*

_____

_____

_____

_____

_____

_____

NOTES: The word "destined" comes from the Greek word **títhēmi**, which literally means, "to place, set, or lay." Figuratively, it means to set, fix, appoint, or determine. God has determined that salvation be found in Christ and His atoning work on the cross. Men may try to earn their salvation by many different methods, but God has appointed only one way—the life, death, and resurrection of Christ.

2. God has determined or appointed the Son as Savior, and it is important to understand that this appointment belongs **exclusively** to the Son. What do the following Scriptures teach us with regard to salvation being found only in the Son?

a. *John 14:6*

_____

_____

_____

_____

b. *Acts 4:12*

_____

_____

_____

_____

c. *I Timothy 2:5*

_____

_____

_____

_____

NOTES: The word "mediator" comes from the Greek word **mesítēs**, which denotes a mediator or arbitrator—someone who brings two adverse or opposing parties together in peace and agreement.

d. *I John 5:11-12*

_____

_____

_____

_____

_____

3. The Scriptures unequivocally state that apart from Christ and His redeeming work on Calvary there is no salvation. This truth has tremendous implications for all men in that the eternal destiny of all is dependent upon how they respond to Christ. What warning is given in the following texts to those who neglect the salvation that God has offered through His Son?

a. *John 3:18*

_____

_____

_____

_____

_____

NOTES: This does not mean that those who hear the gospel and do not immediately believe are condemned to irreversible judgment; rather, it means that those who continue to walk in a hardened state of unbelief will be condemned.

b. *Hebrews 2:1-3*

_____

_____

_____

_____

_____

NOTES: The author of Hebrews is making a comparison between those who reject the law that was mediated by angels (v.2) and those who reject the salvation mediated by God's Son (v.3). If the rejection of God's law brought punishment, how much more the rejection of God's Son!

c. *Hebrews 10:26-31*

_____

_____

_____

_____

_____

_____

NOTES: Verse 26 is not teaching that all but those who have attained sinless perfection are condemned finally to judgment. If that were the case, no one would be saved, because even the most mature believer will still struggle with temptation and sin. The phrase, "go on sinning willfully," is a reference to a continual state of hardened unbelief with regard to the gospel; it is a settled or permanent rejection of Jesus as the Son of God, the Messiah, and the Savior of the world.

Chapter 45: The Son's Work of Salvation
Part Two: The Son's Finished Work

God the Father designed a plan for His people's salvation, and God the Son came into this world robed in human flesh in order to accomplish it. In this chapter, we will consider four important aspects of the Son's work on our behalf during His time here on earth: He emptied Himself, lived a perfect life, offered Himself freely, and rose from the dead.

THE SON WILLINGLY EMPTIED HIMSELF

1. In Philippians 2:6-8 is found perhaps the most powerful description of the incarnation in all the Scriptures. Read the text until you are familiar with its contents, and then explain the meaning of the following sections.

    a. *Although He existed in the form of God, He did not regard equality with God a thing to be grasped (v.6).*

    _____

    _____

    _____

    _____

    _____

    NOTES: The word "form" comes from the Greek word **morphê**, which refers not only to the outward appearance of a person but also to his essential character. The Son did not merely **seem** to be God; He **was** God and was equal with God. The phrase "to be grasped" comes from the Greek word **harpagmós**, which can refer to an unauthorized seizing of something that is prized. The idea communicated is that the Son, through His incarnation, demonstrated His willingness to let go of the privileges of deity in order to do the will of His Father.

    b. *But emptied Himself (v.7).*

    _____

    _____

_____

_____

_____

NOTES: The word "emptied" comes from the Greek word **kenóō**, which means, "to empty or take away." In His incarnation, the Son laid aside the glory and privileges of His deity and became a Man. It is extremely important to understand that the emptying of the Son does not mean that He gave up His deity or became something less than God, but that He laid aside the **glory** and **privileges** that were rightfully His as God (John 17:5).

c. *Taking the form of a bondservant, and being made in the likeness of men (v.7).*

_____

_____

_____

_____

_____

NOTES: The word "form" comes from the Greek word **morphê**, which refers not only to the outward appearance of a person but also to his essential character. Christ did not merely **seem** like a bondservant; He actually and truly became such in every way. The word "likeness" comes from the Greek word **homoíōma**, which may also be translated, "resemblance" or "similitude." Christ bore all the characteristics of true humanity. It was not an illusion—He was a real Man.

2. To conclude this section, we will consider one more text that beautifully describes the Son's incarnation on behalf of His people—II Corinthians 8:9. What truths are being communicated in this text?

_____

_____

_____

_____

NOTES: There was a definite redemptive purpose in the Son's self-imposed poverty. He left the glories of heaven so that we might enter in as sons and daughters of God.

THE SON LIVED A PERFECT LIFE

1. In II Corinthians 5:21 is found an undeniable declaration of the sinless life of Jesus. Read the text, and fill in the blank.

   a. *He K_____ no sin.*

      NOTES: The word comes from the Greek word **ginôskō**, which often bears the Hebrew idea of personal or even intimate knowledge. Jesus did not have even the slightest acquaintance with sin. It was totally and completely foreign to Him.

2. The following verses are also clear proof texts that the Son lived a perfect life. Briefly summarize the meaning of each text in your own words.

   a. *Hebrews 4:15*

   _____

   _____

   _____

   _____

   b. *I Peter 1:19*

   _____

   _____

   _____

   _____

   c. *I John 3:5*

   _____

   _____

THE SON WILLINGLY OFFERED HIMSELF

1. From our study of Philippians 2:6-7 earlier in this chapter, we learned that the Son willingly laid aside the glory and privileges of deity and became a Man. According to verse 8, to what even greater act of humiliation did the Son willingly submit?

NOTES: The cross is arguably the cruelest form of torture ever invented by man. That the Son died willingly on such a cross reveals the extent of His love for the Father and for us.

2. What does John 10:17-18 tell us about the willingness with which Christ offered Himself for the sin of His people?

3. According to Romans 5:7-8, what is one of the most amazing aspects of Christ's offering of Himself for His people?

4. According to the following texts from the Old and New Testaments, what was accomplished for God's people through the Son's offering of Himself?

   a. *Isaiah 53:11*

   _____

   _____

   _____

   _____

   _____

   NOTES: The Messiah will be abundantly satisfied as He reflects upon His redeeming work and the resulting justification of a countless multitude.

   b. *II Corinthians 5:21*

   _____

   _____

   _____

   _____

   _____

   NOTES: Because He became sin on our behalf, we have become the righteousness of God in Him. Our sin was imputed to Him, and He bore the wrath of God in our place. His righteousness was imputed to us, and we stand before God blameless and fully accepted.

   c. *Hebrews 10:10*

   _____

   _____

   _____

_____

_____

> **NOTES:** The word "sanctified" comes from the Greek word **hagiázō**, which means, "to make holy or consecrate." In this context, the word is not referring to the ongoing *process* of sanctification (*i.e.* growing Christlikeness in the believer's life), but to the believer's set-apart (or sanctified) *position* in Christ, which is an accomplished reality. The believer has been made holy before God through Christ's once-and-for-all sacrifice.

d. *I Peter 3:18*

_____

_____

_____

_____

_____

THE SON RAISED HIMSELF FROM THE DEAD

In Chapter Forty-Three, we learned that the Father raised His Son from the dead. However, we must understand that the Scriptures further teach that the resurrection was also the work of the Son. By His own power and authority, He defeated death. The implications of this truth are far-reaching. His power to raise Himself proves His power to raise His people.

1. What do the following texts teach us about the truth stated in the paragraph above—that the resurrection of the Son was a work not only of the Father but also of the Son?

a. *John 2:18-21*

_____

_____

_____

_____

b. *John 10:17-18*

_____

_____

_____

_____

_____

NOTES: The word "authority" comes from the Greek word ***exousía***, which denotes the power and right to act. Because the Man Jesus was also God the Son, He possessed both the power and the authority to carry out His Father's command—to give His life and to take it up again.

2. In John 5:26, Jesus makes a very important declaration about Himself that helps us to understand how He is able to both lay His life down and take it up again. What is the truth being affirmed in this text?

_____

_____

_____

_____

_____

_____

NOTES: This is an exceptionally difficult text, but the truth that is clearly communicated is that the Son, like the Father, has life Himself. The life of even the greatest of creatures is derived: it comes from another (*i.e.* from God). In contrast, the Son's life is inherent: He has life in Himself. Life is a permanent or essential characteristic of the Son.

3. The Son has life in Himself. Therefore, He was able not only to give His life voluntarily but also to take it up again. In the following texts, what are the implications of this truth for those who believe in Him?

a. *John 5:27-29*

_____

_____

_____

_____

_____

b. *John 11:25-26*

_____

_____

_____

_____

_____

NOTES: Christ's power over death has direct implications for His people. Though they die, they will be resurrected to live eternally and will never again be subject to the power or pain of death.

Chapter 46: The Son's Work of Salvation

Part Three: The Son's Present Work

In the previous chapter, we considered four aspects of the Son's work of salvation which He accomplished during His time on earth. However, it is important to understand that His work on our behalf did not end when He ascended into heaven. In this chapter, we will consider two ways in which the Son is still actively involved in the salvation of His people: the Son gives life to His people, and He intercedes for His people.

THE SON GIVES LIFE TO HIS PEOPLE

The life that the Son gives to His people is not confined or limited to the resurrection. He is the source of both our physical resurrection at the end of the ages and our spiritual life and strength in our daily lives now.

1. In John 14:6, Jesus makes a remarkable statement about Himself. What does it confirm to us about His person and the believer's dependence upon Him?

   a. *I am the way, and the truth, and the L_____.*

      NOTES: If Christ is not God, then this statement is blasphemous. Christ is not only the embodiment of God's truth and the way of reconciliation but also the source of all life—physical and spiritual.

2. In John 15:1-8, Jesus makes a similarly remarkable statement regarding His person and the believer's relationship to Him. Read through the text several times until you are familiar with its contents, and then complete the following exercise.

   a. *How does Jesus refer to Himself in verse 1? What does this tell us about Him as the source of the believer's life?*

   _____

   _____

   _____

   _____

b. *According to verses 4-5, how dependent is the believer upon Christ as the source of all spiritual life? Explain your answer.*

_____

_____

_____

_____

_____

NOTES: The analogy is as powerful as it is beautiful. A branch can only bear fruit if it is connected to the life-giving vine. Once it is cut off, it withers and becomes fruitless. In a strikingly similar fashion, the believer can only possess spiritual life and bear fruit through his or her ongoing relationship with Christ, learning and obeying His Word and relying upon His power.

3. To conclude this section, we will consider Paul's confident assertion in Philippians 4:13. What does this text teach us about Christ as the source of the believer's life and strength? How should we live in light of this truth?

_____

_____

_____

_____

_____

NOTES: The word "strengthens" comes from the Greek word ***endunamóō***, which can also be translated, "empowers." It is a present participle, which indicates continuous action. Christ continually gives life and strengthens His people.

THE SON INTERCEDES FOR HIS PEOPLE

Having ascended to the right hand of God, Christ acts as the Advocate for His people, and He lives forever to make intercession before the throne of God on their behalf. Christ's continuous intercession for His people does not mean that He is on His knees before the throne of God begging for mercy on our behalf. Rather, He intercedes as One seated at the very right hand of God, as One who is omniscient and knows every need of His people, as One who has all authority to speak on their behalf, and as One who annuls every accusation against them.

1. I John 2:1-2 is one of the most important texts in all of Scripture regarding the Son's work as our Advocate. Read the text until you are familiar with its contents, and then write your thoughts on the truths revealed.

_____

_____

_____

_____

NOTES: The fact that we have an Advocate before the Father should not make us apathetic about holiness or careless about sin. On the contrary, it should motivate us to obedience because of the great work the Son has accomplished for us. However, the most mature Christian is still subject to moral weakness and sin. Therefore, it is our great consolation that we have an Advocate with the Father. The word "advocate" comes from the Greek word **paráklētos**, which denotes a "helper" or one who is called to speak on another's behalf. The word "propitiation" comes from the Greek word **hilasmós**, which means, "appeasement" or "satisfaction." It refers to a sacrifice given to appease an offended party. The Son is the propitiation for our sins in that He offered His life in our place as a sacrifice for our sin. His sacrifice satisfied the demands of God's justice against us and appeased His wrath. He can be our Advocate and Defender because He Himself has paid for our sins.

2. In Romans 8:33-34, we find another important text regarding the Son's intercessory ministry. What do these verses say is the result of His saving work and intercession?

_____

_____

_____

_____

NOTES: The questions, "Who will bring a charge against God's elect?" and "Who is the one who condemns?" are one and the same. It is as though God were issuing a challenge to every being in the universe, including Satan himself. The reason why no charge or condemnation can be brought against God's people is two-fold. (1) God has justified His people or given them a perfect legal standing before Him. This was accomplished through the perfect life that the Son lived and the death that He died on behalf of His people. (2) The Son now sits at the right hand of God as His people's Intercessor and Defender.

3. In Hebrews 7:23-25, the Scriptures describe not only the power and efficacy of the Son's intercessory ministry but also its permanence. Summarize the text in your own words.

_____

_____

_____

_____

NOTES: This text leaves little to be explained. By the power of Christ's endless life, He is able to save forever those who draw near to God through Him.

4. Although the Scriptures do not reveal the exact nature of the Son's heavenly intercession before the throne of God, some clues may be found in His "High Priestly Prayer," which He prayed on behalf of His disciples during His earthly ministry (John 17:1-26). Below is a list of the petitions that Christ made for His people in that prayer. Match each petition with its corresponding text.

_____ *John 17:11-12*   a. *Christ intercedes for the future glorification of His people.*

_____ *John 17:13*   b. *Christ intercedes for the unity of His people.*

_____ *John 17:15*   c. *Christ intercedes for the sanctification of His people.*

_____ *John 17:17-19*   d. *Christ intercedes for the joy of His people.*

_____ *John 17:21-23*   e. *Christ intercedes for the perseverance of His people.*

_____ *John 17:24*   f. *Christ intercedes for the protection of His people from all satanic forces (see also Luke 22:32).*

Chapter 47: The Spirit's Work of Salvation

In our brief consideration of God as Savior, we must be careful to include the role of the Person of the Holy Spirit. We must never forget that our salvation is a Trinitarian work, involving not only the Father and the Son but also the Holy Spirit. In this chapter, we will learn that He is as essential to our salvation as the Father and the Son.

THE SPIRIT'S WORK IN CHRIST'S ATONEMENT

1. THE SPIRIT CONCEIVED THE SON. The entire work of atonement was dependent upon Jesus' deity and sinless perfection—two facts that make the virgin birth an absolute necessity. According to Luke 1:34-35, what role did the Spirit play in the miraculous conception of Jesus? What was the result?

2. THE SPIRIT EMPOWERED THE SON. Although Jesus was God, He walked upon this earth as a real Man, submitting to the will of His Father and totally dependent upon the Spirit's power. What do the following texts teach us about this truth?

   a. *Luke 4:1, 14*

   b. *Acts 10:38 (see also Matthew 12:28; Luke 5:17)*

_____

_____

3. THE SPIRIT WAS INVOLVED IN THE OFFERING OF THE SON. What does Hebrews 9:14 teach us about this truth?

_____

_____

_____

_____

NOTES: Although it is impossible to understand the full meaning and implications of this text, it is clear that the Holy Spirit in some way aided or empowered the Son in offering Himself on Calvary. Just as the Holy Spirit empowered the Son to live a perfect life and carry out His ministry (Luke 4:18; Acts 10:38), so He empowered Him to offer Himself as an atoning sacrifice.

4. THE SPIRIT RAISED THE SON. The Son's resurrection from the dead was the work not only of the Father and the Son but also of the Holy Spirit. What does Romans 8:11 teach us about this truth?

_____

_____

_____

_____

NOTES: In this text, the primary idea communicated is that the Father raised the Son. However, it is certainly implied that the Spirit is the power through whom the Father raised Him.

THE SPIRIT'S WORK IN CONVERSION

The Scriptures teach that man is radically depraved and utterly dependent upon a work of the Holy Spirit. As we will see below, in order for man to be saved, the Spirit must regenerate, convict, reveal, indwell, and seal.

1. THE SPIRIT REGENERATES THE SINNER. The word "regenerate" comes from the Latin verb **regenerare** [**re** = again + **generare** = to create, beget]. The Bible teaches that man is spiritually dead (Ephesians 2:1-3); he is thus unresponsive to God's call of salvation. In order for man to respond, the Spirit must first impart spiritual life to him. What do the following texts teach us about this truth?

a. *John 3:3-6*

_____

_____

_____

_____

_____

NOTES: The phrase "born again" comes from two Greek words: **gennáō** (to beget, bring forth, or engender) and **ánōthen** (above or again). During the creation of the universe, the Spirit of God was "moving over the surface of the waters," and He brought forth order and life (Genesis 1:2). This same life-giving work of the Spirit must occur within the sinner before he can hear, appreciate, or respond in obedience to the saving message of the gospel.

b. *Titus 3:4-6*

_____

_____

_____

_____

NOTES: Two words are used here: regeneration (**paliggenesía**: **pálin** = again + **génesis** = origin, birth) and renewal (**anakaínōsis**: **aná** = above + **kainós** = new). The importance of the Holy Spirit in the believer's conversion cannot be overemphasized. His initial work in our hearts and minds is the source of our saving response of repentance and faith.

2. **THE SPIRIT CONVICTS THE SINNER OF SIN.** Before the sinner can recognize his need of salvation, he must recognize the gravity of his sin and the judgment that results from it. This is impossible apart from the work of the Holy Spirit. According to John 16:7-11, what is one of the primary works of the Spirit whom Christ has sent into the world?

_____

_____

_____

_____

_____

NOTES: The word "convict" (v.8) comes from the Greek word **elégchō**, which means, "to expose, convict, or reprove." It describes the work of a prosecuting attorney who presents arguments and examples to expose the guilt of a criminal. Though this may seem harsh, it is actually a great demonstration of God's love. Before a man with a deadly disease will seek a cure, he must be convinced of the reality and gravity of his situation. The Spirit convicts the sinner of: (1) his own sin of not believing in Christ; (2) Christ's righteousness, which was demonstrated when God raised Him from the dead; and (3) coming judgment—the cross of Christ resulted in Satan's defeat and judgment and is proof that all who follow him will suffer the same fate.

3. **THE SPIRIT REVEALS TRUTH.** One of the greatest works of the Spirit is that He reveals the Son to sinful men so that they might be saved. What do the following texts teach us about this truth?

   a. _According to I Corinthians 2:10-12, how are the truths of God revealed to men? Explain your answer._

_____

_____

_____

_____

NOTES: The Holy Spirit is the Agent who reveals God's truth to men. However, it is very important to recognize that the Spirit reveals truth to the believer and the unbeliever primarily through the teachings of the Scriptures. He illuminates our minds and enables us to understand what He Himself has written (II Peter 1:20-21).

b. *According to John 16:13-14, what or who will be the main theme of the Spirit's saving revelation to men? Will the Spirit draw attention to Himself or to someone else? Explain your answer.*

_____

_____

_____

_____

NOTES: These promises from Jesus are directed primarily to the apostles, through whom the New Testament would be written. However, we also find truths that are applicable to all believers. Any true work or revelation of the Holy Spirit will always glorify the person and atoning work of Christ. The Holy Spirit will not draw attention to Himself.

4. THE SPIRIT INDWELLS AND SEALS THOSE WHO BELIEVE. One of the most beautiful and powerful truths regarding the Holy Spirit is that He indwells every true believer in Christ and seals us as redeemed children of God. Through the Spirit, the Father and the Son make their abode in us.

a. *What do the following texts teach us about the Spirit's indwelling of believers?*

(1) John 7:37-39

_____

_____

_____

_____

(2) John 14:23

_____

_____

_____

_____

NOTES: The word "abode" comes from the Greek word **monê**, which denotes a room, dwelling place, or place to live.

(3) Romans 8:9

_____

_____

_____

_____

NOTES: This text should not be seen as only a warning, but also as a great encouragement. The Holy Spirit indwells every genuine believer, from the most mature Christian to the most recent convert.

b. *What does Ephesians 1:13-14 teach us about the Spirit's sealing of believers?*

_____

_____

_____

_____

NOTES: The word "sealed" comes from the Greek verb **sphragízō**, which means, "to stamp with a seal or set a mark upon." In the Scriptures, the word is used to denote three ideas: (1) ownership or possession (II Corinthians 1:22; Revelation 7:2-3), (2) security (Matthew 27:66; Ephesians 4:30), and (3) authentication and approval (John 3:33; 6:27). The word "pledge" comes from the Greek word **arrhabôn**, which denotes a deposit, earnest, or advance payment to secure a final purchase (*e.g.* a down payment with the promise of full recompense). The Holy Spirit who indwells, revives, and empowers the believer is also God's seal of ownership and His guarantee of final and full salvation in His presence! Our God is a saving God—Father, Son, and Spirit! The Father, who designed our salvation and governs its every detail, is God. The Son, upon whose person and work our salvation depends, is God. The Spirit, who indwells us and seals us for the day of redemption, is God (Ephesians 4:30). Each Person of the Trinity involved in our salvation is fully God. Therefore, we can have unwavering confidence that the God who began a good work in us will finish it without fail (Philippians 1:6)!

Appendix: The Names of God

WHAT'S IN A NAME?

In the Hebrew culture, one's name is not just a mere title; it is an expression or revelation of the person. In the Scriptures, we find many examples of this: Abraham means, "the father of a multitude" (Genesis 17:5); Jacob means, "one who takes by the heel" or "one who supplants" (Genesis 25:26; 27:36); Nabal means, "fool" (I Samuel 25:25); and Barnabas means, "son of encouragement" (Acts 4:36). All of these names reflect the character of the men who bore them. In a similar manner, the name of God is inseparable from His person and is a faithful revelation of who He is. Each and every name of God expresses some truth about His character.

THE NAMES OF GOD

We will now take a closer look at the names of God. There are no exercises included in this part of our study. Simply consider each name carefully and prayerfully.

God (Hebrew: **El**): The word **el** is one of the oldest and most common names for God employed by Semitic peoples (Babylonian, Phoenician, Aramaic, and Hebrew). The exact meaning of the word is uncertain. It probably denotes power, strength, greatness, and majesty. This name is used 208 times in the Scriptures (Exodus 34:14; Psalm 19:1; Isaiah 43:12).

God (Hebrew: **Eloah**): The exact meaning of the word **eloah** is uncertain. It probably communicates the same ideas as **el**—power, strength, greatness, and majesty. The word occurs 56 times in the Old Testament— including 41 times in the book of Job (e.g. Job 22:12; 27:3; 27:8; 33:12; 37:22; 40:2).

God (Hebrew: **Elohim**): The word **elohim** is the first name of God that appears in the Scriptures (Genesis 1:1) and is used with reference to God more than any other name in the Scriptures (2,570 times). The name **elohim** is probably the plural form of **eloah** and communicates the same ideas of strength and power. In the Scriptures, **elohim** is translated in four distinct ways, depending on the context. The word may refer to: (1) God, (2) gods, (3) angels, or (4) judges. The fact that **elohim** is plural is very important and has two possible interpretations. First, all Semitic languages use the plural to communicate that something is exceptional or unique. For example, a small body of water would be called "water," whereas an immense body of water would be called "waters." The plural word **elohim** is used with regard to God not because there is more than one God, but because He is the great and incomparable God, the one true God above all gods. Secondly, the plural word **elohim** could possibly refer to the plurality of Persons within the Trinity.

God (Aramaic: **Elah**; Greek: **Theós**): The Aramaic word **elah** is translated as "God" in the books of Ezra (4:8-6:18; 7:12-26) and Daniel (2:4-7:28), parts of which were written in Aramaic. The Greek word **theós** is translated as "God" throughout the

New Testament. Neither of the words contributes anything new to the biblical understanding of God. By using them, the writers of Scripture are not affirming the erroneous ideas that the Greeks and Aramaic peoples held about God.

Most High (Hebrew: *Elyon*; Aramaic: *Illai*; Greek: *Húpsistos*): The Hebrew word *elyon* is translated, "Most High," and denotes the exalted state and indescribable majesty of God. In Psalm 97:9, we read, "For You are the LORD Most High over all the earth; You are exalted far above all gods." In the Aramaic passages in Daniel, the name "Most High" is translated from the Aramaic word *illai* (Daniel 3:26; 4:34). In the New Testament, it is translated from the Greek word *húpsistos* (Mark 5:7; Luke 1:32, 35, 76; 6:35; 8:28; Acts 16:17; Hebrews 7:1).

Almighty (Hebrew: *Shaddai*; Greek: *Pantokrátōr*): The Hebrew word *shaddai* is translated, "Almighty," and denotes the infinite power of God. In the Septuagint (the Greek translation of the Hebrew Old Testament), the word is translated, *pantokrátōr* ("all-powerful"). In the Latin Vulgate, it is translated, *omnipotens*, from which we derive the English word "omnipotent."

Lord (Hebrew: *Adon*, *Adonai*): The name *Adon* denotes both lordship and ownership. In the Scriptures, when the name is found in its plural form (*i.e.* *Adonai*), it always refers to God. The plural form denotes intensity—God is the absolute Lord of all things without exception (as with *Elohim* above). The title *Adonai* denotes the lordship of God over all creation. It also communicates a great deal about the relationship that exists between God and His people. As Owner and Master, God is committed to care for His people and provide for their needs. As servants of the Master, we are to be committed to serve Him in absolute obedience. The name *Adonai* appears 456 times in Scripture with reference to God.

Lord (Hebrew: *Yahweh* or *Jehovah*): The name *Yahweh* is the personal name of God and the one most employed in the Scriptures (6,825 times). In Hebrew, the name is written in the form of a tetragram (a word with four letters): **YHVH** or **YHWH**. Although it is not known for certain, the true pronunciation is probably "Yahveh" or "Yahweh." The great majority of Bible scholars believe that the name Yahweh comes from the verb *hayáh*—"to be" (see Exodus 3:14). The name communicates the eternality, immutability, and uniqueness of God. It is important to recognize that the Lord Jesus Christ applied this name to Himself (John 8:58-59) and thus affirmed His own deity.

Lord (Hebrew: *Yah*): The name *Yah* is the contracted form of *Yahweh*. It appears 48 times in the Scriptures, mostly in the book of Psalms and in the exclamation *hallelujah* (*i.e.* "Praise Yahweh!" or "Praise the Lord!"). The word *yah* also forms part of several personal names in the Scriptures (*e.g.* Elijah—"My God is Yahweh" or "Yahweh is God").

Lord (Greek: *Kúrios* or *Kýrios*): For the Greeks, the word *kúrios* could refer to a man of high position and power or a supernatural being (*i.e.* a god). The word is used in the Septuagint (the Greek translation of the Hebrew Old Testament) in place of the Hebrew name *Yahweh* or *Jehovah*, and it is used in the New Testament to communicate the Hebrew idea of God as Lord. The word is employed 640 times in the New Testament as a reference to God. It is significant that the word *kúrios* is used without reservation with reference to Jesus.

Lord (Greek: **Despótēs**): The Greek word **despótēs** denotes ownership and absolute lordship. In its oldest use, the **despótēs** was the master of the house, who ruled with absolute authority. In time, the term developed the negative connotation of someone of unlimited or even tyrannical political authority. However, when the term is ascribed to God in the Septuagint and the New Testament, it communicates nothing negative. God is the rightful Owner and Lord of what He has made. His holiness and righteousness guarantee that He will always use His absolute authority with perfect justice. The term **despótēs** is used 6 times in the New Testament with reference to God (Luke 2:29; Acts 4:24; II Timothy 2:21; Revelation 6:10; II Peter 2:1; Jude 4). In II Peter 2:1 and Jude 4, the reference is specifically to Jesus Christ.

A CLOSER LOOK AT *YAHWEH*

In the following, we will briefly consider the compound names of God that are formed using the name **Yahweh**. Each name will give us greater insight into the person and work of God.

The Lord of Hosts (Hebrew: **Yahweh-Sabaoth**): This name represents God as the omnipotent King and Warrior who rules and protects His people. The word "hosts" may refer to: (1) angelic beings or (2) the cosmos—the sun, the stars, and the forces of nature. The idea communicated is that the Lord rules over all beings and things— earthly, cosmic, or heavenly. He carries out His perfect will, and no one can oppose Him (Psalm 24:10; Isaiah 6:1-5; Isaiah 31:4-5).

The Lord Most High (Hebrew: **Yahweh-Elyon**): This name speaks of the sovereignty, exaltation, and majesty of Yahweh. God is Lord over all, and He is worthy of all worship and praise (Psalm 7:17; 47:2; 97:9).

The Lord Will Provide (Hebrew: **Yahweh-Jireh**): This name was ascribed to God by the patriarch Abraham in Genesis 22:14. In obedience to God's command, Abraham placed his son Isaac on the altar as a sacrifice. Before Abraham could strike his son, God detained him and provided a ram in Isaac's place. The redemption that God provided that day on Mount Moriah motivated Abraham to call the place **Yahweh-Jireh**. Although it is true that God is powerful and faithful to supply **all** our needs, the name **Yahweh-Jireh** is not a promise of economic prosperity; it is a promise of redemption from sin. We ought to die for our own sins (Romans 6:23), but **Yahweh-Jireh** has provided a sacrifice in our place—His only begotten and beloved Son. He is the Lamb who takes away the sin of the world (John 1:29). It is near blasphemy to emphasize economic prosperity over redemption. Jesus did not shed His blood for our monetary gain, but for the salvation of our souls! The redemption of the soul is costly (Psalm 49:8).

The Lord Is My Standard or Banner (Hebrew: **Yahweh-Nissi**): This name was ascribed to God by Moses in Exodus 17:15 after God defeated the army of the Amalekites. In ancient times, the troops would rally together around a standard or banner when preparing for battle. The truth communicated here is that God is the standard of His people. When we rally around Him, our victory is sure.

The Lord Who Sanctifies (Hebrew: **Yahweh-Qadesh**): This name appears for the first time in Exodus 31:13 and several times in the book of Leviticus (20:8; 21:8, 15, 23; 22:9, 16, 32). The word "sanctify" (Hebrew: **qadash**) means, "to separate something (or someone) from common use and to consecrate or dedicate it to some special purpose." The name **Yahweh-Qadesh** communicates many wonderful truths to the people of God. God has separated us from the rest of the peoples of the earth, He has consecrated us for His service, and He is working to conform us to His image.

The Lord Is My Shepherd (Hebrew: **Yahweh-Raah**): This name is found in one of the most well-known and beloved chapters in all of Scripture—Psalm 23. For the people of God, the name **Yahweh-Raah** is one of the most esteemed. God is the Pastor of His people. He loves them, feeds them, guides them, and guards them from their enemies (Genesis 48:15; 49:24; Psalm 28:9; Isaiah 40:11; Ezekiel 34:12; Micah 7:14; John 10; Revelation 7:17). In the New Testament, God is present in Jesus Christ as the Good Shepherd who lays down His life for His sheep (John 10:11).

The Lord Your Healer (Hebrew: **Yahweh-Rafah**): This name is found in Exodus 15:26, where Moses communicates God's promise to Israel: "If you will give earnest heed to the voice of the LORD your God, and do what is right in His sight, and give ear to His commandments, and keep all His statutes, I will put none of the diseases on you which I have put on the Egyptians; for I, the LORD, am your healer." The name **Yahweh-Rafah** assures us that we can trust in the Lord's providential care. He has healed us from the mortal illness of sin; He is also able to heal us physically, and we can trust that He shall do so if, by such healing, His will and glory will be promoted.

The Lord Is Peace (Hebrew: **Yahweh-Shalom**): This name is found in Judges 6:22-24 and communicates one of the most important aspects of the relationship that exists between God and His people—peace. In this passage, Gideon had seen the awesome revelation of God through the Angel of the Lord and is sure that he will die. Such dread is common whenever sinful man has an encounter with the holy God. However, with Gideon and with all of God's people, the grace of God changes such terror to peace. This truth finds its greatest fulfillment in the Lord Jesus Christ, who is our peace (Ephesians 2:14).

The Lord Is Here or Personally Present (Hebrew: **Yahweh-Sama**): This name is found in Ezekiel 48:35, where God promises His presence in the complete restoration of His people in the latter days. The presence of God has always been a very special blessing for the people of God. Adam walked with God in Eden before his fall and judgment (Genesis 3:8). In Exodus 33:12-16, Moses asked that the presence of God might accompany Israel in her journey through the wilderness. In I Kings 8:10-11, God blessed His people by filling the temple with His presence. In the New Testament, the promise of God's presence was fulfilled in its most perfect way through Jesus Christ. In Him, God became flesh and dwelled among men (John 1:1, 14). In the Church, God dwells not only with His people but also in His people through the Holy Spirit (John 14:17). In the consummation of all things, God will dwell with His people in the New Heaven and New Earth (Revelation 21:1-3).

The Lord Our Righteousness (Hebrew: **Yahweh-Tsidkenu**): This name is found in Jeremiah 23:5-6. In this text, God promises that the Messiah will both "save" His people and "rule over" them with perfect righteousness. This prophecy has found its perfect fulfillment in Jesus Christ. Through His perfect life and atoning death, He has made His people righteous, and He rules over them with perfect righteousness. Our righteousness is not our own; rather, the Lord Jesus Christ is our righteousness.

DIVINE NAMES, TITLES, AND METAPHORS

To conclude our study, we will briefly consider the many names, titles, and metaphors that are ascribed to God in the Scriptures. Each name will give us greater insight into the person and work of God.

NAMES THAT REFLECT GOD'S GLORY AND MAJESTY (8)

God of Gods: Deuteronomy 10:17; Psalm 136:2; Daniel 2:47; 11:36
God of Glory: Psalm 29:3; Acts 7:2
God in Heaven Above and on Earth Beneath: Joshua 2:11
Invisible God: Colossians 1:15
Blessed God: I Timothy 1:11
Majestic Glory: II Peter 1:17
Majesty in the Heavens: Hebrews 8:1
He Who Is to Be Feared: Psalm 76:11

NAMES THAT REFLECT GOD'S ETERNALITY (6)

Everlasting or Eternal God: Genesis 21:33; Deuteronomy 33:27; Isaiah 40:28; Romans 16:26
Ancient of Days: Daniel 7:9-10, 13-14, 22
I Am: Exodus 3:13-14; John 8:56-58
Alpha and Omega: Revelation 1:8; 21:6; 22:13
The Beginning and the End: Revelation 21:6
The First and the Last: Isaiah 41:4; 44:6; Revelation 22:13

NAMES THAT REFLECT GOD'S HOLINESS AND JUSTICE (6)

The Holy One: Proverbs 9:10; Isaiah 40:25; 43:15; Hosea 11:9; Habakkuk 1:12
Holy God: I Samuel 6:20
Jealous God: Joshua 24:19
God of Justice: Isaiah 30:18
Righteous God: Isaiah 45:21
Righteous Judge: Psalm 7:11

NAMES THAT REFLECT GOD'S POWER AND SOVEREIGNTY (28)

Creator: Romans 1:25
Architect and Builder: Hebrews 11:10
Possessor of Heaven and Earth: Genesis 14:19, 22
Potter: Romans 9:20-21
Mighty One: Luke 1:49
God of All Flesh: Jeremiah 32:27
God of All the Earth: Isaiah 54:5
God of All the Kingdoms of the Earth: Isaiah 37:16
Mighty God: Isaiah 9:6
Great and Awesome God: Nehemiah 1:5

Great, Mighty, and Awesome God: Deuteronomy 10:17
Great God and King Above All Gods: Psalm 95:3
Great King over All the Earth: Psalm 47:2
Living God and Everlasting King: Jeremiah 10:10
King Eternal, Immortal, Invisible: I Timothy 1:17
King from of Old: Psalm 74:12
King of All the Earth: Psalm 47:7
King of the Nations: Jeremiah 10:7
King of Heaven: Daniel 4:37
King of Kings: I Timothy 6:15; Revelation 17:14; 19:16
Lord of Heaven: Daniel 5:23
Lord of the Whole Earth: Psalm 97:5
Lord of Heaven and Earth: Luke 10:21; Acts 17:24
Lord of Kings: Daniel 2:47
Lord of Lords: Deuteronomy 10:17; Psalm 136:3; I Timothy 6:15; Revelation 19:16
Lord of the Harvest: Matthew 9:37-38
Blessed and Only Sovereign: I Timothy 6:15
Lawgiver: Isaiah 33:22; James 4:12

Names that Reflect God's Judgment and Wrath (7)

Jealous God: Exodus 20:4-5; Deuteronomy 4:24; Joshua 24:19-20
Consuming Fire: Deuteronomy 4:24; Hebrews 12:29
Jealous and Avenging God: Nahum 1:2
God of Recompense: Jeremiah 51:56
Watcher of Men: Job 7:20
Judge of All the Earth: Genesis 18:25; Psalm 94:2
Righteous Judge: Psalm 7:11

Names that Reflect God's Relationship with His People

GOD IS THE ONLY GOD AND CREATOR OF HIS PEOPLE (4)

True God: Jeremiah 10:10; John 17:3
Creator: Isaiah 43:15; 44:2, 21; 43:7
Faithful Creator: I Peter 4:19
Maker: Psalm 95:6; 149:2-3; Isaiah 54:5

GOD IS INTIMATE WITH HIS PEOPLE (10)

Father: Psalm 103:13; Isaiah 64:8; Malachi 1:6; 2:10; John 20:17; I John 3:1
Holy Father: John 17:11
Righteous Father: John 17:25
Father of Mercies: II Corinthians 1:3
Father of Lights: James 1:17
Father of Glory: Ephesians 1:17
Heavenly Father: Matthew 6:14
Father of Spirits: Hebrews 12:9

Abba Father: Romans 8:15; Galatians 4:6
Husband: Isaiah 54:5

GOD IS THE FAITHFUL ONE WHO LOVES AND FORGIVES HIS PEOPLE (9)

God of Truth: Psalm 31:5; Isaiah 65:16
Faithful God: Deuteronomy 7:9
Compassionate God: Deuteronomy 4:31
Gracious and Compassionate God: Nehemiah 9:31; Psalm 86:15
Forgiving God: Psalm 99:8
God of All Grace: I Peter 5:10
God of Peace: Romans 15:33; 16:20; I Thessalonians 5:23; Hebrews 13:20
God of Love and Peace: II Corinthians 13:11
God of All Comfort: II Corinthians 1:3

GOD REIGNS OVER HIS PEOPLE (4)

King: Isaiah 33:22; 43:15
Great King: Psalm 48:2
Lawgiver: Isaiah 33:22; James 4:12
Judge: Isaiah 33:22; James 4:12; 5:9

GOD SAVES HIS PEOPLE (9)

Redeemer: Job 19:25; Psalm 19:14; Isaiah 44:24; 54:5; Jeremiah 50:34
Redeemer from of Old: Isaiah 63:16
Horn of My Salvation: II Samuel 22:3
Deliverer: II Samuel 22:2; Psalm 40:17; Psalm 144:2
Saving Defense: Psalm 28:8
Salvation: Exodus 15:2; Psalm 27:1; 62:1-2; 118:14; Isaiah 12:2
Savior: II Samuel 22:3; Isaiah 45:21; Luke 1:47; I Timothy 1:1; Jude 25
Savior of All Men: I Timothy 4:10
Strength of My Salvation: Psalm 140:7

GOD GIVES SECURITY TO HIS PEOPLE (26)

Rock: Deuteronomy 32:4, 31; II Samuel 22:2, 32, 47; Psalm 62:6-7
Everlasting Rock: Isaiah 26:4
Rock of Our Salvation: Psalm 95:1
Rock of Strength: Psalm 31:1-2
Rock of My Strength: Psalm 62:7
Rock of Habitation: Psalm 71:3
Fortress: II Samuel 22:2; Psalm 71:3; 91:2; 144:2
Stronghold: Psalm 59:9, 16-17; 144:2; Jeremiah 16:19
Tower of Strength: Psalm 61:3
Strong Tower: Proverbs 18:10
Sanctuary: Isaiah 8:13-14
Refuge: Psalm 59:16; 61:3; 62:7; 91:2

Refuge in the Day of Distress: Jeremiah 16:19
Refuge from the Storm: Isaiah 25:4
Hiding Place: Psalm 32:7; 119:114
Dwelling Place: Deuteronomy 33:27; Psalm 91:9
Shade from the Heat: Isaiah 25:4
Defense of My Life: Psalm 27:1
Defense for the Helpless: Isaiah 25:4
Defense for the Needy in His Distress: Isaiah 25:4
Shield: Genesis 15:1; II Samuel 22:3, 31; Psalm 3:3; 115:9-11; 119:114; 144:2; Proverbs 2:7; 30:5
Shield of Our Help: Deuteronomy 33:29
Wall of Fire: Zechariah 2:5
Father of the Fatherless: Psalm 68:5
Judge of the Widows: Psalm 68:5
Strength of My Heart: Psalm 73:26

GOD FIGHTS FOR HIS PEOPLE (6)

Warrior: Exodus 15:3; Isaiah 42:13
Man of War: Isaiah 42:13
Dread Champion: Jeremiah 20:11
Sword of Our Majesty: Deuteronomy 33:29
Consuming Fire: Deuteronomy 9:3
Lion: Isaiah 31:4-5

GOD HELPS HIS PEOPLE (4)

Strength: Exodus 15:2; Psalm 18:1; 28:8; Jeremiah 16:19; Habakkuk 3:19
Helper: Psalm 30:10; Hebrews 13:6
Stay: Psalm 18:18
Very Present Help in Trouble: Psalm 46:1

GOD SUSTAINS HIS PEOPLE (7)

Sun: Psalm 84:11; Malachi 4:2
Shade: Psalm 121:5; Isaiah 25:4
Dew: Hosea 14:5
Fountain of Living Waters: Jeremiah 2:13; 17:13
Life: John 14:6; Colossians 3:4
Light: Psalm 27:1; Micah 7:8; I John 1:5
Everlasting Light: Isaiah 60:19-20

GOD CARES FOR HIS PEOPLE (10)

God Who Sees: Genesis 16:7-14
Shepherd: Psalm 23:1; Isaiah 40:11; Ezekiel 34:11-16
Chief Shepherd: I Peter 5:4
Great Shepherd: Hebrews 13:20
Good Shepherd: John 10:11, 14

Shepherd and Guardian of our Souls: I Peter 2:25
Vinedresser: John 15:1-2
Potter: Isaiah 64:8; Jeremiah 18:1-6
Lamp: II Samuel 22:29
Keeper: Psalm 121:5

GOD IS THE REWARD OF HIS PEOPLE (6)

Inheritance: Numbers 18:20; Deuteronomy 10:9; 18:2; Joshua 13:33; Ezekiel 44:28
Possession: Ezekiel 44:28
Portion: Numbers 18:20
Beautiful Crown: Isaiah 28:5
Glorious Diadem: Isaiah 28:5
Song: Exodus 15:2; Isaiah 12:2

HeartCry Missionary Society at a Glance:

The HeartCry Missionary Society began in 1988 in the country of Peru with a desire to aid indigenous or native missionaries so that they might reach their own peoples and establish biblical churches among them. Since then, the Lord has expanded our borders to include not only Latin America but also Africa, Asia, Eurasia, Europe, the Middle East, and North America.

The goal of our ministry is to facilitate the advancement of indigenous missionaries throughout the world. Our strategy consists of four primary components: financial support, theological training, Scripture and literature distribution, and the supply of any tool necessary to facilitate the completion of the Great Commission.

We currently support approximately 250 missionary families (along with a number of ongoing projects) in over 40 nations around the globe.

Introduction to HeartCry

HeartCry Missionary Society was founded and still exists for the advancement of four major goals:

- The Glory of God
- The Benefit of Man
- The Establishment of Biblical Churches
- The Demonstration of God's Faithfulness

1: The Glory of God

Our first major goal is the glory of God. Our greatest concern is that His Name be great among the nations from the rising to the setting of the sun (Malachi 1:11) and that the Lamb who was slain might receive the full reward for His sufferings (Revelation 7:9-10). We find our great purpose and motivation not in man or his needs but in God Himself; in His commitment to His own glory; and in our God-given desire to see Him worshiped in every nation, tribe, people, and language. We find our great confidence not in the Church's ability to fulfill the Great Commission, but in God's unlimited and unhindered power to accomplish all He has decreed.

2. The Benefit of Man

Our second major goal is the salvation of a lost and dying humanity. The Christian who is truly passionate about the glory of God and confident in His sovereignty will not be unmoved by the billions of people in the world who have "had no news" of the gospel of Jesus Christ (Romans 15:21). If we are truly Christ-like, the lost multitude of humanity will move us to compassion (Matthew 9:36), even to great sorrow and unceasing grief (Romans 9:2). The sincerity of our Christian confession should be questioned if we are not willing to do all within our means to make Christ known among the nations and to endure all things for the sake of God's elect (II Timothy 2:10).

3. The Establishment of Local Churches

Our third major goal is the establishment of biblical churches. While we recognize that the needs of mankind are many and his sufferings are diverse, we believe that they all spring from a common origin: the radical depravity of his heart, his enmity toward God, and his rejection of truth. Therefore, we believe that the greatest possible benefit to mankind comes through the preaching of the gospel and the establishment of local churches that proclaim the full counsel of God's Word and minister according to its commands, precepts, and wisdom. Such a work cannot be accomplished through the arm of the flesh, but only through the supernatural providence of God and the means which He has ordained: biblical preaching, intercessory prayer, sacrificial service, unconditional love, and true Christ-likeness.

4. The Demonstration of God's Faithfulness

The fourth and final goal at HeartCry is to demonstrate to God's people that He is truly able and willing to supply all our needs according to His riches in glory. The needs of this ministry will be obtained through prayer. We will not raise support through self-promotion, prodding, or manipulating our brothers and sisters in Christ. If this ministry is of the Lord, then He will be our Patron. If He is with us, He will direct His people to give, and we will prosper. If He is not with us, we will not and should not succeed. Admittedly, our faith has always been meager and frail throughout the years; but God has always been faithful. As one dear brother puts it: our God delights in vindicating even the smallest confidence of His children.

The Challenge

As Christians, we are called, commissioned, and commanded to lay down our lives so that the gospel might be preached to every creature under heaven. Second only to loving God, this is to be our magnificent obsession. There is no nobler task for which we may give our lives than promoting the glory of God in the redemption of men through the preaching of the gospel of Jesus Christ. If the Christian is truly obedient to the Great Commission, he will give his life either to go down into the mine or to hold the rope for those who go down (William Carey). Either way, the same radical commitment is required.

For more information:

Visit our website at **heartcrymissionary.com** for more information about the ministry—our purpose, beliefs, and methodologies—and extensive information about the missionaries we are privileged to serve.

Made in the USA
San Bernardino, CA
11 March 2020